WOMEN IN COMPUTING

by Judith Morris

G000055299

ComputerWeekly

Published by Computer Weekly Publications
Quadrant House, Sutton, Surrey, SM2 5AS

Publications Manager: John Riley
Deputy Publications Manager: Robin Frampton
Publications Assistant: Katherine Canham

REED
BUSINESS
PUBLISHING © 1989

British Library Cataloguing in Publication Data

Morris, Judith
    Women in computing :
    The Computer Weekly guide to being a business woman in the information technology
    industry.
    1. Women in the computer industry - Great Britain
    2. Women in the computer service industry - Great Britain
    I. Title
    331.4'8100164'0941 HD6073.D372G7
    ISBN 1-85384-004-1

Printed in England by Hobbs the Printer of Southampton

CONTENTS

Chapter 1   Introduction and Overview   1

The computer industry is about twenty years old. So is the 'real' women's liberation movement. Have the two movements benefited each other? Has computing reflected the changing society with which it has grown up? Has the computing industry delivered all the opportunities for women that it seemed to offer when it was first established?

Chapter 2   Education   11

Is the education system preventing more women from getting into technology? A study of universities, polytechnics, teachers, careers officers, WISE (Women in Science and Engineering) and other groups trying to encourage girls to take science and programming courses.

Chapter 3   It's Tough at the Top   23

The success stories and the bad news - women who should be on the board of directors. What does it take to be successful? Sacrifice? Is computing different in this from other industries?

Chapter 4   The American Experience   35

The winners and the losers. Is the US more advanced? How have women got on there? Success in sales and marketing. Opportunities in product development. The UK and the US compared - not all sunshine and dollars.

Chapter 5   Women as Entrepreneurs   47

Women doing it on their own. Sacrifice and success in setting up a company. The pros and cons of contracting.

Chapter 6   Returning to Work   59

Career-breaks and childcare. Women's groups. Home-working and job-sharing. Rest of Europe way ahead of Britain in provision of childcare and other facilities for women - will 1992 lead to a massive brain drain to Europe?

Chapter 7   Problems and Where to Find Help 73

Sexual harassment and lack of co-operation from male colleagues. Professional women's networks and other initiatives. Women in Computing groups. Health problems. Day-to-day problems, e.g. travel, sexism.

Chapter 8   What Does the Future Hold?   87

The factors which make the computing industry seem unwelcoming to women. The need for a change in emphasis. Looking for new ways to encourage women into the industry. A new era in computing?

Appendix 1   The Women into IT Campaign   97

Appendix 2   Useful Names and Addresses   107

Appendix 3   Recommended Reading   111

Index   115

Computer Weekly Publications   121

CHAPTER 1

Introduction and Overview

The computer industry is about twenty years old. So is the 'real' women's liberation movement. Have the two movements benefited each other? Has computing reflected the changing society with which it has grown up? Has the computing industry delivered all the opportunities for women that it seemed to offer when it was first established?

2 WOMEN IN COMPUTING

It is roughly twenty years since the commercial computer industry as we know it took off; it is generally accepted that the same time has elapsed since equal opportunity for women was introduced. It would seem to follow, then, that the growth in the computer industry has mirrored the increase in the status of women at work.

In an ideal world this new, forward-looking industry - the great hope for women seeking successful, rewarding professional working lives - would cast aside old prejudices and distinctions and have as many women as men working in it and contributing to it.

But has that really happened? Over those 20 years the technology industry has advanced like no other; a new generation of millionaires have been born on the back of it. It has transformed the working lives of millions of people, overturned the way world finance is conducted, crept into our homes and schools to change and better the way we live.

The computer industry is run mostly by men and with a staggeringly small number of women in key positions

For women the advance has not been so dramatic, nor so far-reaching. Although changes in the law and in the education system have opened new doors for women, the intrinsic make-up of the computer industry is no different from that of more traditional businesses - run mostly by men and with a staggeringly small number of women in key positions.

In the 1970s, an advertisement appeared in a newspaper in Singapore. It was looking for women to work in the assembly of computer components in a large, unattractive factory. The advertiser was inundated with replies, many of them from the mothers of girls who were eager for their daughters to find a place in the new hopeful society of the future. The advertiser was looking for cheap labour, and for centuries this has automatically meant female labour.

But this story illustrates two points about the position of women in this very modern industry. First of all the response to the advertisement shows the enthusiasm and hope that new technology arouses; but the advertiser's intentions show that however forward-thinking the industry, a woman's place will always be at the bottom of it.

When I was at school a girl, several years older than me, told me that she was not going to university, instead she had found a position 'in computers'. This sounded not only very grand and mysterious - it also sounded very clever. She had secured a job training as a computer operator, a job she did for several years, but today her position is neither grand nor mysterious. She has seen her male colleagues progress to other skilled jobs. The role she occupies in her company (a large multinational organisation) is only slightly higher in status than that of the secretarial staff, whose jobs she scorned when making her career choice.

For centuries cheap labour has automatically meant female labour

No matter how advanced technology is, or how wide the doors of industry have been flung open by that technology, the basic prejudices that have presented a stumbling block to women in many other areas of business remain the same in the computer industry.

CAREER STRUCTURES

Joanna Foster, chairwoman of the Equal Opportunities Board, identified three distinct attitudes in companies towards equal opportunities. Some are instigating equal opportunities at all levels, others are not quite so enthusiastic but are making efforts to modify their old habits, while a third group remain resistant to change. Companies in the computer industry also fall into these categories. But the industry differs from all other industries in one crucial way. It has had the opportunity to help itself by helping women, and in many cases it has failed to do so.

The discrepancies start at the bottom and go straight to the top in the schoolroom and in the boardroom. The education system has not in the past encouraged women to take up what have been termed science subjects, including computing. In the 1970s, the number of women entering the computer industry rose significantly, on a wave of optimism which carried with it people like my school friend. But over the past few years, this number has actually declined. An Information Technology (IT) Skills Agency survey last year found that out of 474 installations the number of women (at 19 per cent) was below the number (20 per cent) in a 1981 survey.

The number of instances of women actually making it to the board are rare

Women represent a respectable percentage of positions in programming, systems analysis and sales (of small systems at least) but the number of instances of women actually making it to the board are rare.

At the same time, the industry is suffering from one of its largest skill shortages ever. Surveys show that the number of trainees in major user installations is more than 3 per cent lower than the number required or planned. The falling birth rate since the 1960s means that fewer school-leavers are joining the workforce, and so employers are finding it increasingly difficult to find the staff they require.

There have been a significant number of campaigns over the last few years aimed at solving this problem, many of them based at school and university level in an attempt to encourage young people to move into technology. The crisis has forced employers to look at neglected or wasted areas of the workforce. In many cases this has meant women. Women leaving school who have in the past been channelled into more 'feminine' jobs; women already in employment who have become stuck in an unpromising position, and women who have left work to have children.

It is a shame that it has taken a crisis of this scale to make employers and industry look again at the wasted resources under their noses. Sadly, it has come rather as a last resort, and many women feel that it is patronising. Also, although the measures themselves are laudable they are, after all, aimed at creating more skilled staff at one level alone, not at appointing more women to senior

The computer industry is no different from any other in the way it treats its female employees

management or educating employers to consider promoting women as rapidly as their male counterparts. The measures have been taken to solve industry's problems by using women; they are not geared to solving women's problems in industry.

I have spoken to many women both inside and outside the computer industry about their experiences. In many ways the computer industry is no different from any other in the way it treats its female employees and the opportunities it offers to them.

What has struck me more than anything is that, in Thatcher's Britain, there are so many female entrepreneurs. Many of them formerly worked in large companies. They left because they could see no way of getting to the top, so they became their own boss.

But not everyone wants or expects to get to the top. Not all working women are the brash, rich 'career' women that the television and newspapers love to portray. Many women do not make any cold blooded choices between marriage and work; work, as to men, forms part of their existence and they want from it the same things that men want - satisfaction, stimulation and a comfortable living.

Many of the jobs that women in technology perform are no more skilled than those carried out by their mothers in the first typing pools. The mystique surrounding the computer industry has fallen away; it has not evolved as a blue-print for industries of the future, with fair and equal opportunities for all. Instead it has fallen into the old traditional divisions that always separated men and women at work - jobs for men and jobs for girls. Women almost exclusively occupy all positions requiring word processing or data entry. It is no accident that in a book on word processing the author refers throughout to executives and managers as 'he' and operators as 'she'.

Women can train as programmers but some of today's programmers are the clerks of yesteryear - keyboard bashers have replaced pen-pushers. Technical jobs requiring engineering backgrounds have, until recently, always been a male preserve. The Women into Engineering initiative was formed to overturn this, and it has been replaced by other lively campaigns to dispel the 'women drivers' syndrome when it comes to technical matters.

GROUPS INITIATING ACTION

Some of the bravest and often most effective ways of making people rethink the way women are introduced to new technology has been carried out by small women's initiatives, many of them in inner cities where unemployment is a problem for men and women alike. They provide help and advice to demystify computing and encourage women to use and learn about computing. What has emerged from their work is that girls - although initially very interested in computing - lose interest at the '0' and 'A' level stage at school. The centres these groups provide encourage them to rekindle that interest.

The British Computer Society's 'Schools Working Party' showed that 51 per cent of those children at secondary school that they interviewed had a computer at home, but by the time they reached the ages of 13 - 15 the number of girls who said they were interested in computers was only 24 per cent.

There are a variety of reasons given for this, not all of them satisfactory. Certainly it would seem that girls are 'put off' using computers at school when they become the preserve of boys playing conflict games. Also computing has been branded as a scientific subject, and so girls at school are less likely to be aware of their potential uses and applications in careers they might wish to pursue.

Steps are being taken all the time to reverse this situation and they seem to be working. Girls are showing signs of genuinely wanting to study engineering and computer science. Employers are speaking very positively about recruiting women and promoting them. People are talking a lot. But something happens inbetween those bright-eyed optimistic beginnings and the published lists of directors of computer companies, or of senior Data-Processing (DP) or IT managers of large

The problems women face cannot just be resolved at the entry-level into industry. They must also be resolved by a good, long look at those at the top

users. Where are the women then? The problems women face cannot just be resolved at the entry-level into industry. They must also be resolved by a good, long look at those at the top.

The relationship of women to computing is not just confined to one of working at the middle level of an organisation; technology has touched the lives of women in many other ways. It is easy to forget the likes of those young women who applied to the advertisement in Singapore - chips and components are still manufactured and assembled in the Third World by rooms and rooms full of exploited and underpaid women.

Many miles away in the sitting rooms of England, women have seized the opportunity offered by technology to combine family life with a job, and have opted to work from home. This has been well documented elsewhere, but it has given a new meaning to 'homework' and provided some hope for the evolution of a decentralised way of working which can benefit everyone.

Although here we are looking at women directly involved in computing, technology has created many peripheral jobs at which women have excelled. These are in areas where women have always been strong - marketing, public relations, administration.

This book looks closely at the experiences of a number of very different women at various stages of their career in comput-ing. The stories they tell speak largely for themselves. What emerges is a picture of intelligent, enthusiastic people who have given a great deal of thought or who have much to offer an industry crying out for new blood if it is to maintain the staggering momentum it has shown over the last ten years.

I have also spoken to many different kinds of employer. Some of the larger computer companies, quite rightly, pride themselves on the policies they have developed to attract women to join the profession. But it is often in smaller organisations that women are given the chance to show how well they can do a job. And it is surprising how many of this industry's most successful women will say that their success is down to 'being in the right place at the right time' or 'being lucky enough to be given the chance'. Few of them cite their own skill, perseverance or tenacity as being instrumental in success. They are all extremely grateful for being taken seriously. Surely that should be their right, not a stroke of luck?

THE SITUATION FOR WOMEN WORLDWIDE

The picture is not necessarily the same the world over. In the United States, for instance, things are a little more hopeful. Women in business are not so much of a novelty, and a woman in a technical position is a fairly common sight. The differences between the way business is done in the UK and the US are too complex to go into, but it is worth saying that it is perhaps no coincidence that initiative is valued highly in the US. In the course of researching

Women are attracted not just by high salaries and the Californian sunshine, but also by more liberal attitudes and the opportunity to rise within dynamic organisations

this book I have meet women who have left the UK as part of a very depressing brain drain to the US, attracted not just by high salaries and the Californian sunshine, but also by more liberal attitudes and the opportunity to rise within dynamic organisations.

All of this sounds very depressing. But it is not necessarily so. The encouragement comes from the women who are quoted in this book; women who have cut a place for themselves in this exciting industry and who will have a place in its future. I do not underestimate their value or their positions. I just wish that there were more of them.

This book looks at the problems, the opportunities, the successes and failures and, hopefully, provides some insight into what can be done by women and for women to make use of the massive potential they have in the industry of tomorrow.

CHAPTER 2

Education

Is the education system preventing more women from getting into technology? A study of universities, polytechnics, teachers, careers officers, WISE (Women in Science and Engineering) and other groups trying to encourage girls to take science and programming courses

There is no evidence to prove that boys are any better suited to computing than girls. But there is evidence that although girls show an early interest in the subject, somehow they lose this interest in their teens and boys take over the terminals.

Great steps have been taken to encourage girls at school to learn about computing. Much of the problem lies in the fact that for a long time computing has not been taught properly in schools - either there was not the right equipment, or the teachers were not trained in the subject and so were uneasy when taking the classes.

Combat games involving firing guns and shooting down spaceships were unattractive to girls

Confusion was exacerbated when computing was dumped in the science and maths curriculum. Much of the time allocated to using computers was left to playing games; nearly always combat games involving firing guns and shooting down spaceships, which were unattractive to girls.

Children are at the mercy of sexist pressures from a variety of sources; from their parents, teachers, peers and of course the media, which has an effect even on children of a tender age through comics and television. Computers and the people who work with them are portrayed as very much part of a male culture.

Luckily, as computing moves out of the laboratory and into the everyday world, an early interest in the subject is not mandatory. A degree in Computer Science is not necessary for a career in computing, and the computer industry is not made up of nutty boffins who have been glued to a terminal screen from the age of three or four.

The problem is to introduce computing as a separate part of a school curriculum, and not an appendage of some other discipline, usually maths or science. In this way girls as well as boys will come to enjoy and respond to the subject and value its importance when the time comes to make a career choice.

Although no-one can change overnight the sexual stereotypes which have developed over hundreds of years, hopefully we can all encourage a maturity of outlook among the next generation which will give them the confidence and information they need to make a balanced judgement about people's roles in society.

After all, most of the people already employed in senior positions in information technology did not have computers at home or at school when they were growing up. Girls should not be 'shut off' computing because they have not followed a scientific syllabus, nor because they have a burning passion for English Literature. Computing, and the people that work in it, are compatible with most interests.

POLYTECHNICS

Pam Morton of Thames Polytechnic, who has championed the cause of women in computing for some years, claims to have gone some way to resolving the problem of attracting girls to the subject through a course she has developed. She noticed a worrying trend in 1979 when 15 per cent of students taking the computer science sandwich course dropped out. The course was aimed at gearing students to the specific needs

Pam Morton of Thames Polytechnic argues that once convinced that they can succeed in computing girls progress extremely quickly

of industry, and a course team dramatically changed the contents of the course without altering that much needed goal.

Surprisingly, when the group of students who had done the new course graduated in 1984, five of the six First Class degrees were achieved by women, as were eight out of the top 12 students overall.

This was a dramatic turnaround. What had happened? Quite simply, the content of the course had changed to increase individual confidence and interest for all of the students, but in particular women had benefited from the new approach.

The course incorporated a new experimental methodology which was based on role playing in computer project teams. The students were shown films and attended seminars on a variety of specialisations from systems design to software engineering. Finally, they had to prepare written reports and deliver them verbally arguing their case.

Pam Morton found that in these situations girls responded much better than boys. They warmed quickly to the idea of teamwork, and students without 'A' levels in computing or science were at a positive advantage in the report writing and research and discussion parts of the project. In fact, large companies like IBM and Conoco Oil have commented on the impressive

Pam Morton contends that the higher the proportion of girls on a course, the better the overall results

presentation put forward by some of the Polytechnic's 19-year-old undergraduates, compared to those of PhD graduates.

'Women have a gift for cooperative working as well as parallel processing and they pay meticulous attention to detail,' said Pam Morton. It is no accident, she claims, that it was a woman who invented parallel processing.

Pam Morton also argues that girls are born managers, and once convinced that they can succeed in computing they progress extremely quickly. 'Men often take up computing because it is a fashionable subject,' she claimed. 'Then they tend to drop out when they discover that it is not for them. But the higher the proportion of girls on a course, the better the overall results.'

The polytechnic approach with its eye decidedly on industry is one route to computing. Sixty per cent of skilled manpower in Information Technology comes from the polytechnics, and Pam Morton claims women make up a much higher proportion (80 per cent) of this figure than that coming out of universities.

Madeleine Walsh was in her fourth year of the course when I visited Thames Polytechnic, and so had already had the chance to put some of the skills she had learnt into practice during her industry year with IBM UK in Portsmouth. She had taken up computing in the Lower IV at school in Liverpool during the first year that the school had run such a course. She did so because she thought it 'was going to be

The girls tend to choose support roles while the boys opt for the more immediately lucrative attractions of contract programming

important in the future' and chose a polytechnic rather than university because she considered the latter to be 'too academic'.

Madeleine said that her long term ambition was to enter management in a technical area. She claimed not to have seen evidence of discrimination during her time with IBM, and so did not foresee any problems.

Sahidah Rashid, in the same year, had also had some experience of computing at her Hertfordshire grammar school, and had chosen a polytechnic for its more practical approach. She was hoping to go into a financial or banking institution in a support role.

The girls, it seems, tend to choose support roles while the boys opt for the less secure but more immediately lucrative attractions of contract programming. Both girls said the equipment they had used at school was, in retrospect, either old or inadequate in some other way, but both agreed that this was irrelevant to their understanding of the subject. There were several other women at various stages of the course, many of whom had not studied computing at all at school. Again, it had not affected their performance or their chances of employment.

One of the most encouraging cases I found in the course was Jane, a 39-year-old ex-social worker who had taken the plunge to go back to full-time education when her youngest child was five years old. She had become interested in the course and the possibilities it presented after visiting a Women's Roadshow, a series of mobile presentations which toured the country about three years ago, aimed at interesting women in a wider range of careers and training. Along with presentations on prospects for women in building, carpentry and architecture was Pam Morton, arguing her case for women in computing.

'Women take things more seriously,' said Jane. 'I thought I was brain dead after five years at home, but I have tried very hard and now have a placement with the Health Authority.'

UNIVERSITIES

Although universities do not provide such direct contact with the world of industry, university graduates are still courted with great enthusiasm by the big computer manufacturers and software houses. Most of them go to considerable lengths to attract graduates, and, aware of the imminent if not immediate skill crisis, are at pains to point out that women are just as important in their recruitment campaigns as men. Carefully photographed brochures extolling the virtues

University graduates are courted with great enthusiasm by the big computer manufacturers and software houses

of working for Bull (previously known as Honeywell Bull) or NCR all show pictures and case studies of smiling and successful women working alongside their male colleagues.

Many of these companies carry out an annual 'milk round' whereby representatives of the firms visit universities and interview students in their final year on the university premises. Applicants who get through the first round of interviews are then invited to a second interview at one of the company's offices. They are often given attitude tests or may have to spend several hours working in teams with other students while being 'observed' and assessed, not just for intelligence but also for their ability to work with others and to a deadline.

For students who have spent their university days wrapped in the world of academia these tests and exercises can be harrowing to say the least. But it is important that computer companies hire the right kind of people, and someone with no work experience and perhaps even an irrelevant degree could well turn out to be the industry's next rising star.

Some large organisations will take graduates from any discipline. But NCR, an international computer manufacturer employing more than 64,000 people worldwide, now only considers students who have studied a degree related to either business studies or computing such as accountancy, economics, business studies, computer science or data processing. Graduates in other areas are only considered if they can demonstrate that they have relevant business experience or a knowledge of the application of computers.

Rex Fleet of NCR says that industry does not sell itself well when people are deciding which courses to take

'We are looking for numeracy, so we tend not to take people from the Arts,' said Rex Fleet, chairman of NCR. 'We work closely with a set number of universities, such as the University of Lancaster.'

Rex Fleet claims that NCR does not discriminate at all between male and female applicants. 'Women are considered as employees, and seen in terms of the job they do,' he explained.

Despite this, the ratio of male to female graduates in NCR is 80:20. Rex Fleet said that even this is higher than in some other companies, and that he would very much like to see the ratio reversed with the 80:20 in favour of women. Women go through exactly the same recruitment process, follow the same graduate training as men and are encouraged along similar career paths. Yet the number of women in the organisation is still very low. Why?

Rex Fleet maintains that women are not attracted to the industry in sufficient numbers. Seventy-four per cent of NCR's workforce are graduates, and the rest are experienced professionals.

'The education system is sound,' he said. 'The universities communicate with business well. But we, in industry, do not sell ourselves at the level when people are deciding to go to university, and selecting which course to do.'

'We have to work very hard to attract the right sort of people and it costs a lot of money. But in the long run it is more expensive to hire experienced people who don't need training, and you don't build up company loyalty that way. Our retention rate is much higher for graduates.'

NCR's extensive graduate training scheme - which starts with a 13-week structured course and 'orientation' period, is followed by formal on-the-job training, and cemented by continuous mandatory courses throughout the graduate's career - is aimed at solving the skill shortage for NCR, and not for the industry as a whole.

Once the company has invested heavily in training the right sort of graduate, it is in its interests to hold on to them. Within six years, a graduate can expect to be a district manager or an equivalent, earning an excellent salary.

Most graduates are steered towards sales. In a sales situation, employees have to be good. 'They can't get away with bluff,' said Fleet. 'I am never conscious when hiring or promoting that women have any more problems in these situations than men.'

On the positive side, Fleet says that slowly but surely the ratio of men to women is changing, and that looking ahead fifteen to twenty years there may well be a much broader mix.

Most other major computer manufacturers tell a similar story about their efforts to recruit female graduates. And their findings are borne out by the universities themselves.

The British Federation of University Women last year passed a resolution at its AGM urging the government to support a campaign to persuade girls and women to enter computer courses at university and also to encourage the colleges themselves to expand these courses, and to include professional skills training in the courses.

The campaign they envisaged would include the provision of funds for more conversion courses for arts graduates who wish to obtain computing qualifications, and the commissioning of careers information about computing specifically targeted at girls to be circulated in secondary schools. This would also encourage industry to support the campaign by giving their female employees time off to talk about their careers at local schools.

The Open University

The Open University has pioneered alternative methods of study and a whole new group of people now have degrees and qualifications who otherwise would have been deprived of them. It, too, has turned its attention to the issue of women in computing.

The Women in Technology project (WIT) began in 1981 as a pilot project, and was so successful that the then Manpower Services Commission funded it for a further six years.

Its aims were, simply, to enable qualified women with relevant work experience in engineering or technology to prepare for a return to work after a career break, to provide educational and career counselling to such women to facilitate their choice of an appropriate Open University technology course, and to promote self-confidence by specially designed weekend courses.

Three years after completing the Introduction to Technology course, about 80 per cent of the women had found technical employment

In 1984 WIT was expanded to include a new option for women without IT experience to study the Open University Introduction to Technology course, so helping women to change career after a career break.

Each year, about three-quarters of the students achieved first degrees in a variety of technical subjects and 3 years after completing the course, about 80 per cent of the women had found full or part-time employment in a technical field. Those unable to find work immediately studied further to enhance their employment prospects, or to ' keep their hand in'.

The Open University system of studying proved to be successful with mothers because, no matter how flexible the hours or even if creche facilities are provided at local courses, there is never the number required to sustain a specialised course at a local level. Studying at home before a return to work is effective and, as the OU notes in its report on the subject, 'valuable national skills are recouped at a modest cost to the nation.'

However, women working or studying at home do not always develop the confidence needed to return to work. The WIT weekends, an integral part of the course, were designed to restore 'professional self esteem', and maintain motivation.

Unfortunately, employers are not always as flexible in their approach to working mothers as the courses designed to help them are

We shall say more about returning to work after a career break later in this book. For the moment, suffice it to say that the only limits imposed on the graduates of courses such as those sponsored by WIT and the OU come from their prospective employers.

Unfortunately, employers are not always as flexible in their approach to working mothers as the courses designed to help them are. Unless education and industry work hand-in-hand, there can be no real solution to the problem.

'The course was invaluable in giving me confidence and updating my technical knowledge. In my field, there is a desperate shortage of good programmers and firms are keen to take women 'returners' to fill this need,' said one former student, now working as a computer programmer with Mobil Data Services.

'Mobil have offered me a 20 per cent reduction in hours to fit in with my children's requirements. I plan to stay with Mobil who are keen to keep me and are willing to give me more flexible hours in order to do so.'

If only all employers were so far-sighted!

ALTERNATIVES

The traditional education pattern for a professional job, consisting of 'A' levels, university or polytechnic and then graduate training scheme, cannot always be enjoyed by everyone. And there is some evidence that it does not always produce the kind of staff the industry needs; certainly at the moment, it is not providing the numbers.

But women are very resourceful - and it not really surprising that where no training facilities have existed for women at a local level, women themselves have established them.

Elsewhere in this book we shall be examining the work carried out by women's groups to educate and encourage women of all ages to train in computing and secure jobs in the industry.

CHAPTER 3

It's Tough at the Top

The success stories and the bad news - women who should be on the board of directors. What does it take to be successful? Sacrifice? Is computing different in this from other industries?

There are few large computer companies which can boast a ratio of computing personnel which is greater in favour of women than 80 men : 20 women. But the women who have made it in such organisations tend to be successful, confident and capable. But what exactly are they doing, and how did they get there?

Data Logic employs 826 people in the UK, 160 of which are women. Of these, 70 are technicians and related managers, 30 are administrative staff and managers, and 60 are secretaries.

It is not realistic to include secretarial staff in the number, as the jobs done by these women are not radically different from those carried out by secretaries working for non-computer companies. Of the remaining 100, women are employed in a variety of roles, but only one is a director.

A MARKETING SUCCESS STORY

Flick Willetts, marketing manager with Data Logic, is unusual in that at 43 she has 20 years' experience in the computer industry. She started with an Industrial Mathematics degree from Leicester Polytechnic, at the time a new course, and the forerunner to computer science. When she left she became a computer programmer, writing in machine code on an early STC machine, back in 1962.

'I dropped in, very fortunately, at the beginning of something,' she said. 'Very few people understood what we were doing, which gave me a very good feeling. But I don't think I had any idea then what the impact of computers would eventually be.'

In those days, when Flick went for interviews for programming jobs, she was asked some fairly odd questions, such as the one from the interviewer who wanted to know if she could knit. 'The logic was that if I could master a complicated Fair Isle pattern, then I could understand computing!' she recalled.

Knitting has played little part in Flick's career, which has included some highly technical jobs at the forefront of computing. She spent considerable time in the late 1960s in the United States, working in both public service and for a large retail organisation as a senior analyst and programmer. When she returned to the UK, however, prospects were not so rosy; the US

'I became known as the one who fired the drunks! I just couldn't stand seeing people who were doing nothing'

were investing heavily in new technology and then, as now, had a much keener commercial eye than the British.

Flick found work with the National Children's Bureau, which was conducting social and medical research into children born in 1958. Flick took four years to mastermind the massive project, which she did from initial design to implementation. But when the project was complete, and she took a job with the rapidly expanding Michelin company, she discovered the complicated world of office politics which surrounds large organisations.

'I arrived and found that I didn't really have a job to do,' she recalled. 'I sussed then that you have to be self-motivated in a company like that. So I found myself a desk and set myself up as a source of authority on implementing software. It was my first taste of real management, and I became known as the one who fired the drunks! I realised then that I just couldn't stand seeing people who were doing nothing.'

'I had no management training as such, and it was unusual for a woman to be in a management position then. I had to fight to establish myself as a real person, although I never really came across any prejudice. It was made easy for me because I was seen to be slightly different anyway as I had worked abroad, and came from London.'

It was then that Flick discovered true ambition. She split up from her husband, left Stoke-on-Trent, and joined Data Logic in Birmingham as the most senior woman there. Unfortunately, the first job she was given was, she believed, at a much lower level than it should have been. On her second day in the job she told her boss that it was not for her. It took a long time, nearly a year, for Flick to persuade the management that she was capable of better things. But eventually she got her break.

'I gave the boss a hard time,' she said ruefully - and relocated to London after a spell with Raytheon in the US. There she began working with Unix and had the exciting task of trying to make it more friendly, which culminated in the launch of a Data Logic product which effectively solved the problem of making the system more commercially useful.

Why, then, did she choose to move out of the technical field into marketing?

'The move to marketing meant taking responsibility,' she explained. ' Technicians say "Why don't they do this or that?" They themselves don't take any responsibility. And I was also getting fed up with the stereotyped greasy-headed image the technos had. I wanted to move into professional services.'

Grabbing Opportunities as they Appear

'I learnt very much as I went along, and made some terrible mistakes. But once again, I got in at the bottom rung and climbed my way up, I have learnt to see opportunities and grab them.'

In the years since she started her career, Flick has seen a change in herself. She has gone from going to work, drawing her money and paying the bills to someone who looks for job

'I would have got my boss's job if I had been a man,' she said. 'But it is me, and not the environment that is at fault.'

satisfaction, and enjoys knowing that she has a role to play. The skills she possesses, she claims, are her ability to communicate and organise. She is also hardworking and committed. 'I would have got my boss's job if I had been a man,' she admitted. 'But it is me, and not the environment that is at fault. Women's expectations are lower, so we don't push for the big one like men do.'

These days, there are more girls entering Data Logic than when Flick first started off in computing. She says that she always wants to recruit more women, and graduate women prove to be excellent when interviewed.

'There are less of them, but the few that do come through really stand out, and they are always good. It's a tough course for graduates at Data Logic. The men tend to be more aggressive and defensive. Women are not as afraid of appearing foolish, not frightened of asking questions, and that's how you learn.'

THE PERSONNEL ROUTE TO THE BOARD

Sally Smedley is a rare breed, a woman director. She has been with Data Logic for four years, and now sits on the main board. However, her relationship with computing is not a technical one, as she came up through personnel. She came to Data Logic from DEC, and she came highly recommended.

'At my interview, my boss said two things,' she said. 'He said "I wish you were a fella, and I wish you were from IBM".' Being unable to do much about either of these evident shortcomings, Sally got the job as Company Personnel Manager and two years later became Personnel Director. Not having a technical background, in Sally's opinion, has proved to be a positive advantage in an organisation staffed with technicians.

'At first,' she explained. 'There were a lot of mutterings of the 'What does she know?' variety but not any more. I was always honest, and have a lot of skills which are different from many of those used by other people in the company, but they are just as important.'

'At the outset I knew nothing about computers,' she admitted. 'I was in a company making tin cans before I went to DEC! But the prospect of working in a new industry was very exciting. I don't really need to know the nitty gritty of computing in my job, but I do need an understanding of customer needs and strategic and technical terms and how we acquire them.'

> 'A lot of women are their own worst enemy. I've fought to get where I am. Not many women do that.'

'I can analyse situations and recognise what needs to be done. A lot of women are their own worst enemy. I've fought to get where I am. Not many women do that.'

So where do they go wrong? Sally claims that many women are not prepared to stand up and risk being crushed, although women, she says, unlike men, are capable of being tough and sensitive at the same time. 'A lot of men aren't that tough,' she said. 'Sometimes it is just bravado, just ego.'

Her own brand of toughness and ambition has meant some degree of compromise in her life. She has been married twice and, at 38, has no children. Her husband does not work and the pressures of her job - when we met she had visited New York four times in the previous two months - put considerable strain on her marriage. It is difficult, but it is what she wants.

> 'Men get things more easily than women. You have to stick your neck out, and it's not always easy.'

'I have been very single-minded,' she said. 'I wanted to be as successful as I possibly could. I've thought through my career path very carefully and taken advantage of all my opportunities to achieve my own goals.'

'The computer industry offered me an opportunity I had not found elsewhere,' she claimed. 'I feel that it does not draw upon traditional areas of prejudice and discrimination.'

In the next two years she will, she feels, reach a crossroads where she will have to work out what she wants to do next. She pursues her goals aggressively, and makes no apology for putting herself first every time she has to make a choice.

'Anyone who says that someone else comes first is a liar and a fool,' she stated.

'Men get things more easily than women. You have to stick your neck out, and it's not always easy.'

EMPLOYER ATTITUDES TO WOMEN AND WORK

Most major computer manufacturers and software houses claim to have a positive attitude to the employment of women. Bull, for example, has an equal opportunities policy which states that while recognising that it is difficult for women to combine what it calls 'home management with business management' - although many women would argue with that - the company can go some way to helping female employees by providing guidance and counselling, flexible working hours where appropriate, and keeping in touch with women at home on both a formal and informal basis.

One of the company's publications featured an article two years ago about women in the company, in which one of its successful women employees was quoted as saying that 'simply by being here I have proved that feminism is unnecessary' - by which she presumably meant that there are no barriers to women of the right calibre. In the same article, another woman is quoted as saying that 'personally I don't think it is any company's responsibility to make it easier for women to combine families and work - they certainly don't do it for men.'

Employers want women to return to work after they have had children, not because they are enlightened, but because they need the staff

Here speak, however, women who have already achieved success in their chosen fields without too much difficulty. We would not expect Bull to quote dissatisfied or disgruntled women who had been passed over for promotion in its own in-house publications.

It is also interesting to note that the inference is that the company is doing women a favour by re-employing them, or letting them design systems at home. It is the sign of a good employer, along with things such as the provision of BUPA or profit-share schemes.

These days the attitude has shifted slightly. Employers want women to return to work after they have had children not because they wish to appear enlightened or responsible, but because they need the staff.

At Bull's Hemel Hempstead establishment, there is a unusually high number of women managers, and the company is very proud of this, although it cannot really explain why all these women have found themselves at the same location. Despite the company's statement on helping with flexible

In computing, sexism is often experienced at the customer end of the job

working hours and so on, all of the eight managers at Hemel are full-time and have either grown-up children, or none at all.

Bull does, however, run a 'Homeworkers' scheme which helps technical women with experience to work on the design of systems from home, with the option to rejoin the company full-time in the future. At the moment the scheme only employs a handful of women, but there are women within the company who would like to see the scheme extended to include the possibility of part-time work, too.

Most of the women managers at Hemel - in resource management, personnel, product and project management - have a science background and all claim to have suffered little if no prejudice in their careers, at least not from their employer.

It does seem that sexism is something which is experienced at the customer end of a job in computing, or so the computer companies would have us believe. Customers are surprised, initially, that a woman has been sent to them to resolve a problem or sell a product, and sometimes think they are being sold short. It is here that a woman must excel; all of the women who have been in this position agree that if they appear anything less than faultless it is almost impossible to maintain any professional credibility.

A company must be convinced of a woman's skills and expertise. A mediocre male employee can invariably get by

No-one is more aware of this than the employer of women, so it goes almost without saying that a company must be completely convinced of a woman's skills and expertise before exposing her, and the customers, to such a situation. A mediocre male employee, however, can invariably get by.

For a woman working for herself the problems are even greater. She has to get into the site in the first place, without the backing of a large, well-known organisation behind her.

GOING IT ALONE: CONSULTANCY

Christine Newman is a consultant specialising in data administration, and has seventeen years of DP experience, including a job as general manager of a major software vendor, MSP. She has no degree, but went straight into DP as a trainee programmer with Imperial Tobacco. She claims that her decision not to go to university was the right one.

'My boss at Imperial thought that a degree would be an advantage in getting into management. But I proved him wrong. There was actually a slump in the industry at the time I would have left, whereas I got a foot in the door before it happened.'

She progressed through the usual professional channels, through analysis and programming, and, because she was employed by a go-ahead firm, became involved in a variety of things, particularly database and data dictionaries, which has been her passion ever since.

After eight years as general manager of the software company she decided to leave and get back in the field as a consultant.

'It was not a sudden decision,' she claimed.'One of the things I found as a manager was that I got further and further away from field work. I realised that I had a lot of skills to offer that were being used less and less. So I took the plunge to go back into the field, but as a specialist on how to implement a data dictionary in practical terms.'

Like most successful women, Christine has found few problems now that she is established, but encountered several when she was younger

When we spoke, Christine has been in business five months and had already found that work was coming to her, and that she was being approached directly. She had also recently got married, which she claimed provided her with a 'safety net' in going it alone.

Like most successful women, she has found few problems now that she is established, but encountered several when she was younger.

'I had to prove my credibility,' she explained. 'I had several major battles with employers in the early years, and it is all to do with how you are perceived by management. I got on well with them, but the leap into management is much more difficult for women.'

'I was the first woman to go on a Player's management course, and I was lucky in having a good start to my career. MSP was very positive about women in the company, but I could still walk into a major presentation and be met with total disbelief that I could do the job. You have got to win them over in the first five minutes, and if you do, women do have certain distinct advantages.'

'I do think things are changing now. At one time I used to present in a DP environment and the people there would be 98% male. But over the last few years there have been a noticeable number of women in the audience who have good technical positions, but sadly few of them are managers.'

CHAPTER 4

The American Experience

The winners and the losers. Is the US more advanced? How have women got on there? Success in sales and marketing. Opportunities in product development. The UK and the US compared - not all sunshine and dollars.

Although the British have an international reputation for excellence in the fields of technological research and engineering, it is the United States of America that has really capitalised on the success of the computer revolution. In the sunny valleys of California live the dollar millionaires, the large multinationals, the start up one man-and-a-dog firms that have progressed from garages to international success stories.

Many believe that the Disneyesque rags-to-riches syndrome could not happen here, in our land of tradition and class snobbery. Until very recently the quickest way up the corporate ladder was via the right school and accent. Certainly the US does not have the same rigid class distinctions that we still hold in the UK, and in many ways the Americans do have a more liberal attitude when it comes to rewarding merit and recognising and encouraging talent from every quarter.

But have women in computing fared better than their British sisters? In many ways the answer is yes. There are more female directors in the US, but then of course the US is a much bigger country. And if the business is competitive here, it is much tougher across the Atlantic. Despite their reputation for open-mindedness in business, the Americans do not always promote women as promptly as men. And sexism, like racism, is an irrational human attitude that afflicts people all over the world.

Sexism, like racism, is an irrational human attitude that afflicts people all over the world

SUCCESS IN MARKETING IN THE US

Liz Richell is vice-president of marketing for California Software Products, a company founded in California which sells Baby 34 and Baby 36, products which allow IBM mainframe software to run on personal computers. Liz, now in her early 50s, is the first to admit that America was, for her at least, a land of opportunity.

'I had studiously avoided ever learning anything about the computer industry,' she admits. 'When computer people got together, I found that they tended to speak in zeros and ones, which to me were quite unintelligible and boring!'

Liz was educated in her native England, with an emphasis on the predictable secretarial and business skills. She joined a photographic studio and became involved in selling. In the late 1950s Liz and her husband (who are now divorced) decided to pack up and travel the world. They ended up in the United States, and she found herself spending the next two decades raising four children. But towards the end of this period, Liz set up her own small company as a sideline, selling photographs from her friend's studio in England to calendar and book publishers in the US. Divorce eventually meant that Liz had to look for more serious and lucrative ways of earning a living.

Like so many successful women, Liz Richell puts her achievements down to being 'in the right place at the right time'. Few men, however, would say that their achievements were down to luck

She joined Manpower Temporary Services interviewing and placing office staff, and it was through this job that she met up with an old friend, who told her he was looking for a personal assistant. Liz promised to find him one, but he ended up rejecting all the candidates she sent to him, and he offered the job to Liz instead.

'Enter Liz Richell into the computer software business!' she recalls. 'At the time California Software Products designed mini-computer software languages, a scientific database management system, a text editor etc. We were about fifteen people, and daily life hummed along pretty well. But I was bored.'

'Then at about the same time that the idea for Baby 34 was mooted, the marketing vice-president left the company. Baby 34 was a unique product and created a lot of excitement within the company. But as company funds were mainly being used for development, there was little left to hire outside help, so I was given the task of attracting publicity.'

So Liz designed advertisements, a monthly newsletter, brochures and fielded dozens of questions a day. In 1985 Baby 36 was introduced, and now the systems are installed in over 15,000 sites worldwide. The company has grown and is represented in 36 countries, with subsidiaries in Toronto and Slough. Liz is vice-president of marketing for the firm.

'I did not bring to this position the kind of background that would be expected,' says Liz. So what did she bring?

Liz Richell, like so many successful women, puts her achievements down to being 'in the right place at the right time' and is grateful to her boss for 'giving her the opportunity' to show she could do well. On the other hand few successful men would say that their achievements were down to luck. So there must be more to it than that.

'I don't scare easily,' she admits. 'And I'll take on anything. At first I thought computers were boring, but computing is like any other business and getting into and helping to run a company that is growing quickly is very, very exciting. There is not a day that I don't look forward to my work, and we are always doing something new.'

As a woman, and an older woman at that, Liz claims that she has never encountered any problems.

'When I was first in the industry, there was a great imbalance of men to women. Today if you visit a trade show, for example, the numbers are almost equal.'

'We have a lot of women in the company, but that is nothing to do with me. I'm not a women's libber. I look at what people can do, and the candidate with the best qualities fills the vacancy.'

'When I first came to the US, there were a lot more opportunities than in the UK. But I don't think that this is still the case. We had no problem at all finding a UK office, and I think things are actually a little easier in the UK.'

But Liz admits that she would not have progressed in the way she has if her children were still young. She works a seven to 11 hour day with international travel and frequent dinners with clients. She has to be always available.

'I've never kept regular hours,' she says. 'I'm not a structured person. But I am happy here. I love living in California, and I am very at home with the company. We are all good friends, and it is tremendous to work with people you like and respect. And at the moment the company is a good size, big enough for gossip, but not big enough for politics.'

SALES AND MARKETING: OPPORTUNI-TIES IN THE US

Ann Ferguson has had a different experience. She is married to Bob Ferguson, a software 'guru', and between them they run ANSA, a US-based company developing compilers for IBM systems. ANSA, too, has a UK office. Ann, originally from the UK, feels that women are much better treated in the US.

'There are a lot more women at the top. Although, four or five years ago, 20 women executives were interviewed, and recently the same women were re-interviewed. Fifty per cent of them have abandoned their careers because they just couldn't get to the top. That's very frustrating.'

Like Liz, Ann does not have a lot of sympathy with women who 'give up'. She claims that women are 'not that put upon anymore.'

But in her own job she has experienced what it's like for women in other parts of the world. 'The Japanese don't speak to me,' she says. 'If I make a remark at a meeting, they act as if I hadn't said anything, and wait for a man to speak. We have distributors in Venezuela and Latin America, and there women are third class citizens. In the Western world, however, women should have no trouble at all.'

'You have got to study and learn - things change so fast that you just have to keep up.'

The education system in the UK is, Ann believes, superior to that in the US, and she also maintains that there are opportunities here for women if they take them.

'You have to get into the industry,' she says. 'I started selling in 1980 and gradually learnt about computers. Now I know all about the insides of IBM Systems 34 and 36. You have to specialise these days - new things are happening all the time. We're in this business because no-one else is.'

'I know the industry, the market, the systems. I can't write the code, but I'm the best we've got when it comes to marketing and selling. I'm good at dealing with difficult customers. You have to be technically competent, but you also have to be diplomatic. We give 24-hour support worldwide in German, French, Spanish and Italian.'

'I like to work,' she says. 'I work weekends, and I suppose I'm a slight workaholic. But I'd also like to be replaced, so that I could do something else. A lot of running a business is tedious, I'm the bad guy - the one who always get elected to blast someone else.'

'But I've learnt a lot about marketing and advertising, I'm open-minded. I listen to other people. Computers have a dull image, but dealing with people is always rewarding. And if people are happy, that means productivity.'

Even Ann's idyllic house in the mountains, that she designed and built herself and is only half-an-hour from the ski-slopes, is on line to the office. But what advice does she have for women starting out in computing?

'There's no mystique attached to the computer,' she says. 'And it helps to get a good basic understanding of a computer. There's a lot of hogwash surrounding computing - you have to be able to discern who's right and who's wrong. You must read a lot, to stay abreast of the industry and to get ideas about the different areas of computing. You have got to study and learn - things change so fast that you just have to keep up.'

SUCCESS IN PRODUCT DEVELOPMENT

Marylin Bohl, who used to be vice president of product development for Digital Research (DR), is a shining example of how expertise and potential can be recognised and developed. After graduating in maths from college in 1964 Marylin worked in a variety of programming positions but was 'impatient - I wanted to be at the forefront of technology'.

She joined Bull, and was presenting a paper on Fourth Generation Systems when an IBM boss who had been listening came up to her and asked her if she had ever wanted to work for IBM. She said yes, she had, but IBM had said that it didn't need her. The man from IBM said, 'oh yes it did', and

Marylin joined the company where she spent her first year writing a book on computer concepts.

Marylin then worked in database and data communications until she entered management in 1975, responsible for IBM's data management system, IMS.

In 1979 IBM introduced DB2, a new relational database for mainframes, and until last year she was in charge of that product, with 140 people answering to her, and with total responsibility for the development and introduction of the product. She developed the database strategy for the IBM corporation, and set the standards for the quality of the product.

'In the end I had everything going like clockwork,' she says. 'And I was looking for a challenge. I was by then very visible in the marketplace, and a lot of companies came to me and offered me positions. But I didn't want to go into competition with my own product.'

The perfect opportunity came when Dick Williams, who she had worked with at IBM, invited her to join Digital Research, a much smaller company, and where, she says, 'everything I do makes a difference.' She has a world-wide position for product development and also product marketing responsibility for the entire DR line.

'My emphasis is on product strategies. I am building DR as a company. The basic skills that I used at IBM are the same, but here we focus on microcomputing, whereas at IBM it was mainly mainframe work. I have a responsible position, and basically the company succeeds or fails with me.'

'Women have to prove themselves more than men. Women have to prove that they can do whatever needs to be done.'

Marylin agrees that there are few women, in the US and elsewhere, that have attained similar positions. She claims that the one thing needed is a sound technical background. She herself has written nine books on technical subjects which are used in colleges and universities all over the world, and worked a '20-hour day' for DR.

'Women have to prove themselves more than men,' she says. 'Women have to prove that they can do whatever needs to be done. I have not set goals in my life and gone all out to achieve them; I have simply responded to the challenge, and IBM management recognised what I could achieve. It is the same at Digital Research.'

Looking back, Marylin thinks that the decision to join a manufacturer - IBM - was a key one. And being given the opportunity to research and develop relational database really gave her a chance to show what she could do. The decision to leave IBM and go to DR was, she says, another important move.

'DR is not just one more company,' she explains. 'With our graphic capability we can apply factors to develop real-time systems with graphics which don't exist today.'

'I don't know about the future,' she says. 'I may want to be president of a company one day, but I would have to spend 75 per cent of my time with dollars and cents, and I wouldn't be able to get my hands dirty working with the technology. It's fun advancing technology and seeing it applied effectively - it's fun, fun, fun.'

Obviously few women - or men! - have Marylin's natural ability and exceptional skills. But she claims too, that any young woman starting off in computing needs to arm herself with as much technical know-how as possible.

'And it is also important to understand the computer industry - how technology is issued and where the opportunities lie. You have to keep your eyes and ears open to what is happening in the industry. You have to talk to people in the industry. Communication is an all-important skill; it is vital in this business.'

'You have to keep your eyes and ears open to what is happening in the industry. You have to talk to people in the industry. Communication is an all-important skill; it is vital in this business.'

'For women, the ability lies in seeing a way to get on, seizing an opportunity, and letting others see how good they really are!'

'And my motto,' she adds, 'is don't make enemies, never build yourself up to show the other guy up - see a problem as "our" problem; work with people, and don't go in for fingerpointing people. If you work to win, men don't see you as competitive, because if you win, everybody wins.'

US AND UK EXPERIENCE COMPARED
Life is not all Sunshine and Dollars

For these three women, the US has proved a land of milk and honey. But there are opportunities in this country too, and of course throughout Europe.

The United States has in the past attracted many people in information technology, both men and women, but Silicon Valley (as the area in California which gave birth to so many successful computer companies has come to be known) has proved to be a tough place to work and live. In the last few years as many small firms have fallen by the wayside as have hit the big time. Life is not all sunshine and dollars.

The UK has not suffered in the same way, and a certain degree of caution when approaching something new has, in this case, proved to be no bad thing. Yet the UK has really only one computer manufacturer, ICL, and if you walk into any computer installation many of the systems you will see are not UK made or developed. And yet this country boasts some of the finest innovative brains in the world.

CHAPTER 5

Women as Entrepreneurs

Women doing it on their own. Sacrifice and success in setting up a company. The pros and cons of contracting.

One of the characteristics of the computer industry and its various spin-offs has been the prevalence of small, start up companies that have mushroomed as a result of the computing boom. Many individuals saw opportunities, took them and established successful companies themselves, or, unfortunately, fell by the wayside and have never been heard of since.

In Thatcher's Britain the entrepreneur has found much encouragement. Why work for the Big Boss when, with a good idea, some backing and a business head on your shoulders, you can work for yourself?

Computing has lent itself to the self-employed dream. The increase in the power of microcomputers and their lowering price has brought them within the pockets of a whole generation of new users. The rapidity with which they started to sell created numerous gaps in the market which small companies were quick to fill.

The urgent need for skilled programmers and software personnel also meant that people with these skills found themselves in an enviable position; they could work where they chose and, within reason, name their price. Many went into business selling nothing but themselves as contract programmers - they had all the advantages of full-time, lucrative employment with the freedom of being self-employed.

Although it is a generalisation, women have traditionally tended to put security before money and there are perhaps fewer self-employed women than men. But there is a surprisingly high number of women who have 'gone it alone' - broken away from the organisations they worked for and set up companies of their own. The reasons for this are many, but it is no coincidence that a large proportion of women who have become their own bosses did so when they realised they would never become bosses by any other means.

Women are good managers, good business people and invariably possess most of the practical skills necessary to run a business. But it is often only when they set up in their own businesses that they get the opportunities to show what they can do. Branching out on your own requires a lot of confidence, but you also need the ability to convince others to invest in your idea. It is not always easy.

SACRIFICE AND SUCCESS IN SETTING UP A COMPANY

Daphne Gordon is managing director of High Integrity Systems (HIS) in Hertfordshire. HIS is a computer systems house specialising in scientific and industrial applications which require reliability and continuity of operation; it is also the leading European source of expertise and development support for Ada in embedded applications. Ada is the standard programming language for defence and aerospace projects.

Daphne discovered at an early age that she was good at science and mathematics, and took a Computer Science course over 20 years ago when there 'were not many other women, but enough not to stand out like a sore thumb'. She started working in her holidays at Elliot Automation, where she returned upon graduating. She worked on radar systems, air traffic control and other real time systems with a mathematical bias, progressing from a junior programmer, to programmer, and then from systems analyst to systems designer. She stayed with the firm for five years.

'People didn't chop and change jobs so much in the late 60s,' she says. 'I worked shifts, earned good money and learnt a lot, which is the best thing about any job.'

Most women, claims Daphne, have their critical stage, when their career comes to a crossroads. Hers came in the shape of her divorce, when she decided to move away from Elliot - by that time owned by Marconi and she joined ITT at a time when the company was full of electronic and mechanical engineers.

'Microprocessors had just arrived - people were saying, "What is this thing called software?" I knew what software was, and so I was able to say, "It's straightforward".'

Daphne started to develop software for telephone exchanges and other high profile areas; as every year went by she moved further up the management ladder, she travelled the world for ITT and 'thought nothing of hopping on a plane for Stuttgart one day and turning up in New York the next.'

'It is easy for women to invite problems by doing unprofessional things. It drives me mad to see women go to pieces, or burst into tears. I understand then how many men feel about it.'

She coped with the massive task of keeping up with the changing technology and passing the information on to other colleagues. Did she ever encounter any problems because of her sex?

' There may have been times, but if so I was unaware of them,' she admits. 'I certainly never lacked appreciation in terms of pay rises. With women, people don't let you forget it if you make a mistake. You have to try harder, and you just do it without thinking about it.'

'It is easy for women to invite problems by doing unprofessional things - some women can be silly. It drives me mad to see women go to pieces, or burst into tears. I understand then how many men feel about it.'

At this point in her career, a group of four (male) colleagues told Daphne that there was the opportunity for the five of them to make a real go of a business. They plotted and planned in their own time for a year, and then offered the business to

ITT, asking them to fund the idea with up to £100,000. ITT thought about it for six months or so, and the group heard nothing.

'The five of us decided not to do anything, but then I resigned, so the others resigned and we all left in the summer of 1981.' For the first three months of HIS's life, everything was done by committees, even making the coffee. It soon became obvious that things were not going to work out.

'All the money was going out, we spent money on salaries, we had an overdraft and I couldn't sleep,' remembers Daphne. 'So I said right. we'll do it my way, or I'll go. They said OK, and that was that.'

Looking back, Daphne says that those first few months were incredibly hard work. But now HIS is worth £10 million and is still growing at a rate of 50 per cent a year.

'Once you have money, you can generate more,' she explains. 'Now we have more money per employee in the bank than GEC. Now 80 per cent of the company is owned by City institutions, so therein lies the rub - I can't retire! The City invests in people and only trusts certain people.'

It helps to have someone on the board who has some contact with the decision makers at the top, especially in a sensitive area such as defence. Luckily, Sir Frank Cooper, ex-head of defence procurement, became chairman of HIS which helped the company find the credibility it needed. He believed, as does Daphne, that smaller companies were not getting a big enough bite of the defence cherry. He knows the ins and outs of the political game.

Daphne feels that things are difficult for small companies, especially in terms of cash flow in the crucial first few years. Hard sales people are vital, she says, if you are going to make money. 'The one thing I would do differently with HIS if I were to do it again,' she admits, 'is to make sure that we had sales and marketing skills from the very beginning as well as sound technical skills.'

Daphne is also convinced of the strength of her company's product, Ada, which she is sure will replace the commercial language Cobol by the mid-1990s. 'Cobol is already long in the tooth,' she claims. 'There are millions of dollars invested in Ada, and Cobol itself started out in the US Department of Defense, and grew into a commercial language.'

Certainly so far her vision has been proved right and her business is successful and profitable. But she does not underestimate the commitment needed.

The Need for New Horizons

'I have worked from six in the morning until nine at night,' she says. 'I have worked nine days a week for the past eight years. It destroys marriages, it meshes everything together. Priorities have to change. You have to be tough on others, and tough on yourself. And four days out of five I enjoy it. I would never say I enjoy it five days out of five, because I don't believe anybody who says that about their job.'

Brutally honest about herself and about life, Daphne Gordon is the first to admit that twenty years in any business is a long time. And she feels ready now to leave it.

'This is an industry I would not have missed out on for the world,' she says. 'I developed a real taste for it, although I had no idea when I started that I would eventually do something like this. It is a very dynamic industry. You have to run fast to keep up with it. But the company I set up now runs quite happily - they can manage without me and now I want to travel, see the world, play tennis, do all those things I have planned to do for years and have always put off doing. I want to do it before I reach 100 - after all, at the end of the long day, you have to ask yourself 'Did I enjoy it?''

Her advice to young women starting off in computing is simple. 'Take every opportunity you can to learn. If you are offered an opportunity, don't turn it down. Most of all, women have to feel happy about themselves.'

> Take every opportunity you can to learn. 'If you are offered an opportunity, don't turn it down.'

CONTRACTING

As the computer industry's need for skilled staff increases, many companies choose to employ contract staff as a short-term solution to the problem, or to carry out special projects for which they have no in-house expertise.

Contracting is an interesting and often financially rewarding way of working. As we have discussed, many feel that women prefer the security of working for one employer, but this is by no means exclusively true.

Many women who have reached a certain plateau in their career elect to do contract work and develop their career in that direction rather than stay with one company, or even a variety of companies, and rise within a structured career pattern. Instead of going into management positions, which as we have already seen is not always easy for women to do, they take a sideways step and use their skills as contract staff or consultants.

> Good contract staff are like gold dust to some employers, especially if they have solid experience and specialist computing knowledge

There are many agencies which specialise in placing contract staff, and most of them have a good reputation with both workers and employers. Not all contracts are short-lived, either. Some of them can last for months, even years. One Recruitment Agency, Computer People, say that the average length of a contract is 39 weeks.

This way of working provides the contract worker with a wide variety of experiences and allows them to develop skills in many business environments. Good contract staff are like gold dust to some employers, especially if they have solid experience and specialist computing knowledge. Nearly all computer users these days use external staff in one way or another.

The Computer People Group is one of the largest contract agencies. Before placing staff with a company, it analyses the needs of the organisation concerned, and if consultants are needed, it will bring in project managers, consultants, specialist technicians or even entire project teams, many of whom have worked together before and so know each other's strengths and weaknesses in a working situation.

Consultants or contract staff operate as independent business people. When they embark on an assignment, contracts are drawn up between the individual and the agency, and the agency and the client company. The individual is paid for the work done, and is paid directly by the agency.

First time contract people usually opt to have PAYE deducted at source at first, but if they choose to make consultancy a career, many form their own Limited Company, where the individual is responsible for her own tax and National Insurance payments, in the same way as a freelance or self-employed person.

Time off can be taken between contracts, for an extended holiday, to look after children, or even to pursue another interest

Contract staff or consultants come from a variety of back-grounds. The skills they have developed usually reflect those that are in the most demand in the industry, but management skills and a professional attitude to the job are as important as programming and systems analysis expertise.

Computer People provides a handbook called *Professional Conduct* for all its consultants which gives useful advice on some of the difficult situations that can some-times occur at locations where staff are assigned, such as relationships with client staff (some permanent staff at a client site may be resentful of contract consultants, claims the book, perhaps because they believe that interesting project work is being given to outsiders, or perhaps because of a difference in earnings).

Contract work provides a happy medium between full-time permanent employment with one company, and the rather alarming prospect of going it completely alone

The book also covers confidentiality, industrial relations problems, general conduct and absence. Naturally, high standards of professional conduct are vital for both consul-tancy and consultant.

There is an increasing number of women working as consultants for Computer People and the consultancy claims that the figure is considerably higher than a few years ago. The company itself is doing a great deal to attract women to the profession through its own literature and in recruitment.

In a recent survey conducted by the company, three women working as analysts were interviewed and the main problems they identified were the inevitable long working hours and, to a certain extent, the detachment that a contract worker must employ, although one woman claimed that this was a positive advantage. 'I loathe office politics,' she said. 'I let permanent staff sort that sort of thing out.'

Pressures on contract staff are perhaps more intense than on permanent employees; work needs to be done quickly. A great deal - often miracles - is expected of consultants who have often been brought in at great expense and as a last resort to solve an urgent problem. Days off and holidays may not be as easy to arrange as before. Most things have to fit in with the timetable of the client's project. Women with sick children who are forced to take time off from a project may find themselves in a difficult position, although most reputable agencies organise sickness payments.

But the advantages of working as a consultant are attractive. Time off can be taken between contracts, either for an extended holiday or to look after children, or even to pursue another interest. There is a great deal of variety and excellent opportunities to increase experience and work with a range of different companies and people. There is obviously a great deal of satisfaction in seeing a project through from beginning to end; in solving a problem and making calm out of what is often chaos.

For women, consultancy work has an additional advantage. As one analyst programmer working for Computer People pointed out; 'Companies employing contract staff are prepared to pay a lot of money for both men and women, and treat them equally. They are paying for the skills, not the individuals.'

Marie Evans is a 37-year-old business analyst working as a consultant for Computer People. She decided to enter the computer industry after 13 years of working as a secretary, and took a programming and systems design course in Sydney, Australia.

She enjoys her work in consultancy; especially the process of bringing information together. 'Business analysis is fascinating,' she says, 'as it is surveillance of market activity.'

Marie sees her career developing as she learns more about the technical nature of her job and new developments which affect it - such as looking into different methodologies for analysis and learning about new databases - rather than moving into management. 'I don't like managing people,' she says.

Contract work provides a happy medium between full-time permanent employment with one company, and the rather alarming prospect of going it completely alone, either with a small business or a financial partnership. Consultancy provides the security of regular work, with variety and flexibility of working.

CHAPTER 6

Returning to Work

Career-breaks and childcare. Women's groups.
Home-working and job-sharing. Rest of Europe
way ahead of Britain in provision of childcare
and other facilities for women - will 1992 lead to
a massive brain drain to Europe?

There was a time when it was considered reasonable at job interviews to ask a woman applicant if she was considering marriage or children. If she said yes, the interviewer would put a black mark against her. For many years employers shied away from taking on even the most promising female candidates for fear that they would leave after a few years, never to return.

Thankfully, that question is no longer acceptable. On the contrary, we are approaching the day when women attending job interviews can confidently quiz a company about the provision it makes for women in terms of maternity leave, mid-career breaks, childcare facilities and retraining.

Britain lags behind most of Europe in its provision of child-care facilities, and in the general encouragement it gives to women who want to return to full- or part-time work

There is such a drastic shortage of skilled personnel at the moment that many computer companies are slowly beginning to realise that women form an important part of the workforce. But as well as attracting women into the industry, they must also find ways of holding on to experienced women already working for them.

It is a fact of life that many women who have built up a successful career leave, often at the peak of their career, to raise a family, and only a proportion of these women return to work. They do not necessarily return to the same company, and they often find that there are many financial, emotional, and practical difficulties associated with returning to work.

This country lags behind most of Europe in its provision of childcare facilities and in the general encouragement it gives to women who wish to return to full or part-time employment. But slowly and surely, changes are coming about, although most of these are through private schemes rather than government-sponsored initiatives.

WOMEN'S GROUPS

For some years now, a group of senior women managers at ICL have been getting together once a quarter. At first there were only 25 of them, but the figure has tripled over the last three years. All of the women are in management grades, and although originally very low-key, the 'Thursday Club', as it is known (the women wanted to choose a name that gave nothing away) is now company supported.

The group is a business-oriented one, and invites speakers from both in and outside the company to address relevant business issues. The women have found the club a useful way of forming contacts and, although they have avoided women-only issues, ('The last thing we wanted to do is attend a women's group') they have recently accepted that they have a responsibility to increase the number of women in the company and help those women succeed, and they have decided to be more active in that area.

> ICL's policy is one of 'positive action, not positive discrimination'

Last year the group ran a workshop in conjunction with the Pepperel Unit of the Industrial Society where they looked at the problems facing women and formulated a document which was presented to the management, listing ways by which the number of women in computing could be increased.

Elizabeth Lank, Human Resource Manager for ICL and for other STC-owned companies, said that many male managers were, in some ways, keener on the idea of helping women to get on than their female counterparts. Some women, she explained, took the attitude, 'I didn't get any help, why should they?' However, Elizabeth was at pains to point out that the policy is one of 'positive action, not positive discrimination.'

At about the same time, the Women into IT group approached ICL and the company contributed to the feasibility study which researched ways of making women more interested in computer studies and helping them to choose computing as a career.

The range of facilities that the ICL working party listed as a result of their workshop encapsulates the various areas which must be attacked if women are to return to work. As Elizabeth Lank pointed out, it is very much an all-or-nothing situation. Each of the elements help the others. A piecemeal approach will have few benefits. Unless all of the factors are taken into consideration, little can be achieved. What good would it be to retrain women if no provisions are made for flexible working? What good are childcare facilities if women are not given adequate career-breaks?

CHILDCARE

There is little provision for pre-school child care in the UK. Most women who return to work after having children have several limited options. They can choose a private nanny to look after their child. A live-in nanny - one who is provided with accommodation and food, and often even her own car - can expect to be paid about £40 a week. A daily nanny - one who comes to her employer's home each day but lives out can expect between £100 to £150 a week in London. The employer also has to pay tax and National Insurance for the nanny.

There are a number of state nurseries but places in these are few and far between, and usually reserved for families with problems

Some families share nannies, which reduces the cost but means the children have to alternate between two homes. This scheme is also unpopular with nannies, and with an increasing number of women returning to work, good nannies are hard to find.

Au pairs or mothers' helps are cheaper, but are not qualified to look after small children, and au pairs are only allowed to work a few hours a day, as the main purpose of their time in the UK is supposed to be educational.

Alternatively, registered childminders will look after children while their mothers are working. Childminders are other local mothers and, although not qualified, they are approved by the social services, who also provide a list of contacts within your area. Childminders cost between £30 and £50 a week, and will look after other people's children as well as your own. The child has to be taken to the childminder's home each day, and collected, and childminders do not usually like taking on very young babies.

There are a number of state nurseries but places in these are few and far between, and usually reserved for families with problems. Private nurseries exist but these, too, are difficult to get into because of their scarcity. They are expensive - about £100 a week - and, again, there are very few that have facilities for small babies.

Women who have family or friends nearby can sometimes come to some arrangement with them. Otherwise their options are as described above. It is not an attractive picture.

Workplace nurseries are provided by some companies, and this is a system which is being looked at by many others, but there are few in existence. Some of the large banks operate them in London. It is a big step to take for an organisation: the set-up costs are great as not only is space required but also qualified nursery nurses have to be employed in the legal child-to-nurse ratio.

Those companies that have introduced workplace nurseries tend to pay the set-up expenses and subsidise some of the cost, with the parents paying the rest. Companies also have to know that the nurseries will be used, not just in the short-term, but in the future. Consequently a great deal of research has to be done to establish just how many women have children or how many are considering having them, and if they would use the facilities if they were available.

The working party at ICL in charge of looking at child-care facilities has visited and studied workplace nurseries. Its intention is to draw up a process for different offices to implement, and to run a pilot process in a key skill shortage area. Over 900 people have been sent a questionnaire asking questions such as what current child-care arrangements are, how much would parents be prepared to pay and so on.

Unfortunately, the British Government's view is that workplace nurseries are a taxable benefit, and individuals are therefore taxed for using them

Workplace nurseries have their drawbacks. Women who commute long distances to work may not wish their children to make that journey every day. The government's view on workplace nurseries is, unfortunately, that they are a taxable benefit and individuals using them are therefore taxed.

Nurseries cost at least £100,000 to set up and run, and a company cannot reasonably expect to recover more than 40 per cent from parents. It is an expensive solution, and although parents on the higher salaries might find the system cheaper than, say, employing a private nanny, ICL wishes to extend the service to secretarial staff, who would not be able to afford as much. Another option would be to charge on a sliding scale according to salary.

The Campaign for Workplace Nurseries will act as a consultant to firms considering this option, and, for a fee, will carry out most of the organisational work involved.

Another option is for companies to subsidise child care facilities nearer to the parents' home. This again requires great organisation and administration, but it is a system which companies who value their female employees are studying.

Elizabeth Lank pointed out that because of all these problems, convincing the company of the feasibility of such systems is not easy. The way to do it, she suggested, is to address the problem as a business problem and not a personal issue.

'A lot of managers have a very traditional view of how women should be,' she said. 'Their wives have always stayed at home with their children, so they will poo-poo any ideas aimed at encouraging other women to leave their children and return to work. You have to come at them with a business argument; say to them "Look, I don't care about your wife, this company is short of skilled staff and if we don't keep these women our competitors will get them".'

Elizabeth Lank is convinced that this is the only viable approach. 'It would not have got us anywhere to get into this as a women's issue. The present publicity has helped, and given the whole argument a credibility. Suddenly it is a business issue. Eighty per cent of labour force growth over the next five years will be women.'

CAREER BREAKS

The idea of a long mid-career break does not lend itself to the computer industry. As we have already heard from many women quoted in this book, the computer industry changes so quickly and technological developments evolve at such a rate that even six months away from the business is a long time.

But this is not to say that time spent away from the job cannot be used effectively and, in the long run, turn out to be advantageous to the individual and to the employer.

'Five years out does not help anyone,' said Elizabeth Lank. 'But a two year break, with training and some related study, or flexitime working or homeworking, could do.'

'We would try to counsel staff to return to work as soon as possible but we would also have facilities that they could use if they wished to stay at home longer, that would enable them to stay in touch and keep their hand in.'

Women who take time off to have children often experience a crisis of confidence on their return. Months, even years, spent playing with children is not the ideal way to prepare for a serious business meeting or wrestling with a difficult problem. But increasingly, women can be counselled before their return and there is an ever-growing number of courses which will renew confidence, instil enthusiasm and prepare individuals for work.

Training is a vital part of returning to work and no-one would expect a woman to step back into a pressurised job without a period of study and acclimatisation

Training is a vital part of returning to work and no-one would expect a woman to step back into a pressurised job without a period of study and acclimatization.

Legally, a woman is entitled to 11 weeks paid leave before the date her baby is due and 29 weeks after the baby is born, if she has worked for the firm for two years. Women who have not been working for their employer for two years or who are self-employed are entitled to benefits - Statutory Maternity

Pay or Maternity Allowance - both of which are much lower than most salaries.

However, many employers are beginning to take a more sympathetic approach to women who require maternity leave but have not worked for the statutory two years. In a highly mobile industry such as the computer business, many employees leave their jobs before two years and there is increasing pressure on employers to make exceptions to this rule in the case of valued employees.

Unfortunately, many of the benefits and systems described here are only available from large, responsible employers. Women who work for small firms which do not have the money or resources for child-care or extended leave, often cannot offer the same level of support. Women who have set up their own companies have to find their own ways of marrying work with a family.

There are a number of groups and organisations, listed at the back of this book, which aim to help women in these circumstances and put them in touch with others in the same situation.

HOMEWORKING

Homeworking is not a new option for women, especially in the computer industry. The power and reliability of microcomputers is such that a great deal of highly skilled work can be carried out away from a central office, and even transmitted to that office from remote locations by a telephone link. Technology is now at the stage where homeworking is part of many people's lives, be they men or women, parents or not.

F International was one of the first companies to pioneer the idea of homeworking, and is staffed almost entirely by women working from home, carrying out programming, systems analysis and other professional work. Most of the staff work on specific projects and attend meetings and briefings, and are sent on training courses and seminars, much as any other type of professional worker. The main difference is they are free to carry out the bulk of their work at home, in their own time.

Founder Steve Shirley (the first woman President-Elect of BCS) set up the company many years ago because she saw that there were a number of women who wished to look after their families but who also needed the stimulation of satisfying work. At the same time she saw that women who left work when they had families, simply because they had no alternative, formed a much wasted resource in an industry crying out for experience and skill.

ICL has used women outworkers for eighteen years. Originally called the 'Pregnant Programmers', the group now employs women who are neither pregnant nor necessarily programmers

ICL's CPS division has also used women homeworkers for 18 years. Originally called the 'Pregnant Programmers', the group now employs women who are neither pregnant nor necessarily programmers. The scheme has been so successful that the division's Sue Halbot acts as a Remote Working Consultant, selling her services to other companies who wish to explore this way of working.

The management skills required for homeworking are very different from those usually employed in computer companies. Managers have to learn to judge on output, not what time someone came into the office that morning.

'You need trust, organisation, and the ability to set clear objectives and goals - really the basic managerial skills that we should all have anyway,' said Elizabeth Lank. 'It requires a very high calibre of manager.'

ICL is considering building something into its management training programme which would help managers cope with these new ways of managing staff. There are, naturally, gender differences in management style and those too will be built into the courses.

'Women have very effective leadership skills but they don't use them in the same way as men,' said Elizabeth Lank. 'They tend not to act as "bosses". We are using women managers to "mentor" other women to help them with these problems and also some of the political problems associated with working for a large company.'

New ways of working include flexible working hours, where an employee can choose her own working hours , part-time working, job-sharing and homeworking

As demographic influences change the patterns of our working life, so alternative ways of working emerge that do not fit into the nine-to-five office-bound image that for many years we have associated with a professional job.

This is good news for women who would find it impossible to have children and pursue a career in the traditional way. Some of these new ways of working include flexible working hours, where an employee can choose her own working hours to suit herself and her lifestyle, part-time working and job-sharing as well as homeworking.

PART-TIME WORK

Many companies say that women who work part-time put more into their two or three days a week than most full-time employees put into a five-day week.

Hopefully this is not the main reason for making part-time work available, but it is at least an encouraging indication that part-time work, once very unpopular with employers as it usually meant hiring two sets of staff for one job (and that meant two sets of tax and National Insurance contributions) is gaining favour again. Certainly most women with families find part-time working the most attractive option.

JOB-SHARING

Joh-sharing has become reasonably popular in certain types of work. British Telecom has just opened up 200,000 jobs to job-sharers. Job-sharing is just that - two people share one job, taking exactly half of the salary each and carrying out the job's duties on a week on/week off basis, or in some other way suitable to the company and to the nature of the job.

Job-sharing only works under certain circumstances. The job which is shared has to be of a type which can be easily handed over without too much explanation or confusion. In this way a professional job which is tackled in an individual way cannot easily be taken over by someone else and carried out successfully. Also, people tend to be proprietorial about their work and do not always like to think that someone else can simply pick up their pieces and lay them down again without any problems.

But all these new ways of working should be discussed. Personnel departments are beginning to learn that there can be no clear statements of policy as to what a firm will or will not accept. If women come to them with problems, they should be creative about the solutions, and adapt the company's resources to accommodate the individual's requirements.

'One woman came to us,' said Elizabeth Lank, 'who wanted to take time off. She wasn't having a child, she just wanted to take some time out to do other things, but she still wanted to keep her job open. It was discussed, and we agreed to her request. There has to be changes in personnel policy. We have to approach these problems with an open mind.'

WHAT DOES THE FUTURE HOLD?

As we move towards 1992, and the opening up of the European market, working practices are bound to change. The rest of Europe is way ahead of the UK in terms of child-care and other provisions for women workers. With the increased mobility that 1992 will bring, will women choose to go to, say, Sweden to work and have their children, because of the superior facilities available there?

The UK cannot afford to lag behind any longer - there are bound to be statements from Brussels on the subject soon and there is a government commission actually looking at childcare at the moment. Hopefully we can avoid a massive brain drain to Europe.

But the publicity that the shortage of skilled workers has received and the consequent new interest in encouraging women to return to work could itself have serious repercussions.

As we have seen, it has taken a serious industry dilemma to make employers look to women as the answer to their problems. The shortage has been caused not only by a lack of trained computer professionals but it has been exacerbated by the population drop in the 1960s and 1970s.

In twenty years' time, things such as child-care, flexible working options and career-breaks could be as much a part of our working lives as company cars and subsidised cafeterias are now

We are now experiencing a reversal of that phenomenon, and currently there is a baby boom again. This means that in twenty or so years' time there will be no labour shortage; in fact there may very well be the opposite.

What will happen then? Will employers decide to take away the facilities they have made available to women now? It is worth noting that the best childcare facilities this country has ever known were introduced during the war when women were needed to carry out men's work while they were away fighting. When the war finished and the men came home, the nurseries were closed.

In twenty years' time things such as childcare, flexible working options and career-breaks (for men and women) could be as much a part of our working life and the benefits an employer provides as company cars and subsidised cafeterias.

With more women in strong management positions by then, the decision to keep or lose such facilities will ultimately rest with them.

CHAPTER 7

Problems and Where to Find Help

Sexual harassment and lack of co-operation from male colleagues. Professional women's networks and other initiatives. Women in Computing groups. Health problems. Day-to-day problems, e.g. travel, sexism.

Although employers are trying hard to attract women into the computing industry, there are still many problems faced by women, even when they have succeeded in their fight to win a position in which they can prove their skill.

In a recent survey, over 40 per cent of women said that they had experienced sexual harassment of some kind during their working lives. Women also encounter sexual prejudice, ridicule and lack of co-operation from colleagues while trying to do their job.

In many offices there are poor facilities for women, and women who need to travel alone in the course of their job experience a variety of situations which their male counterparts do not.

In the computing world in particular, there have been a variety of health scares for women which many employers do not take seriously. There are also numerous difficulties connected with raising a family and maternity leave, for which there are some solutions which we have examined elsewhere in this book.

So do women need nerves of steel, a hide as thick as a rhino's and a will of iron to overcome all these problems and carve themselves even an averagely successful career in today's so-called 'modern' industries?

Some would say 'yes'. But there is really no need for women to face this catalogue of disastrous situations. Luckily, the world of business is beginning to realise that just as women can do as good a job as men, they also bring different skills and qualities to the job, and require different management.

Many of the women quoted in this book went out of their way to stress that they were 'not feminists' and that they did not want to be seen as part of a 'women's group', or as women doing what they were doing for a 'women's cause'.

This is understandable. Feminism, to many people, smacks of an alternative, political, left-wing way of thinking which is anathema to big business. If a woman tries to make a political point, not just for herself but for other women, she is accused of being a feminist, a loony not to be trusted and certainly not a person to be taken seriously.

It is interesting that at ICL the working party set up by Elizabeth Lank focused its arguments on business problems, with conditions to encourage women to return to work being used as the solution to these problems, not as facilities to help women *per se.*

As Elizabeth Lank pointed out, the issue is such an emotive and personal one that this is the only way to approach the problem. And yet we live in a world where it is accepted that women should run entire nations - not just Margaret Thatcher, Indira Ghandi, Golda Meyer, Corazan Aquino and Benazir Bhutto - Britain also has a female monarch.

But when it comes to running companies - or even a small part of a company - a woman in charge is still treated with suspicion. She may, God forbid, staff the entire organisation with other women, taking men's jobs and create an uneven society where women hold the balance of power!

A recent report concluded that women find verbal sexual harassment offensive, but 'in the current labour market, they no longer have to put up with it'

This may raise a laugh but it is a very un-funny fact that just as men do not, even today, trust a woman behind a wheel they do not trust her behind a desk. One successful managing director was informed by financial advisers, when her firm was looking for a Stock Market listing, that her company would not be taken seriously by The City without a man at the helm.

Another was told by her board of directors that she must represent the company at an important international conference. Although her male colleague was the obvious choice, she was asked to go instead of him because of the novelty value a female delegate would give her organisation at a male-dominated convention. Needless to say the woman in question was a particularly attractive blonde.

There is a certain pathetic inevitability about these situations which many women have come to accept as an occupational hazard. An article in *The Times*, which quoted a 1987 survey of 157 workplaces by the Labour Research Department, involving 46,000 employees, found that three-quarters of the staff said they had experienced sexual harassment, and two-thirds said that they thought the problem was under-reported. The article finished by stating that women find verbal sexual harassment offensive but in the 'current labour market, they no longer have to put up with it.'

But many women do put up with it, either because they do not want to acquire a reputation for being a trouble-causer or a strident feminist, or because they do not know how to prevent it.

Only a quarter of the workplaces surveyed by the Labour Research Department had any specific agreements to deal with these problems. Most trade unions have a process for handling sexual harassment, as should most personnel departments.

However, problems of a not-too serious nature can often be resolved in numbers. More and more women are finding help and support from groups. Groups, clubs and networks (the golf club, the all-male drinking club, in modern times even the squash club?) have long been used by men to establish contacts, forge deals and lay claim to promotions. But the women's groups that exist - whether formal or informal - are not trying to mimic the 'old-boy' network.

The Thursday Club at ICL has been mirrored by a group of much younger women, new graduates, who meet regularly to discuss such problems and who have found ways, between them, of diffusing difficult situations and discussing ways of avoiding them.

If, however, there are no such groups within a company there are now an increasing number of organisations which women can join which offer support, contacts and training.

PROFESSIONAL WOMEN'S NETWORKS

Women in Management is, surprisingly perhaps, celebrating its twentieth anniversary in 1989 which shows that the concept of the woman as manager is not a new one. It has 800 members and is aimed at all women who manage, either in business or public service, or women who are planning a career in management. It offers a variety of opportunities for members to meet other women and runs seminars and courses on training and development, running a small business and changing career.

The Women Returners' Network was set up in 1984 and its aims are both national and international. It promotes education, training and employment opportunities for women returning to work, and provides information for employers about schemes available to facilitate the retention and re-entry of female employees.

Its initiatives have included conferences about managing career breaks run jointly with the Industrial Society's Pepperell Unit, and the publication of guides to educational and vocational courses available to women returners in

England and Wales. Its members include representatives from industry and commerce, the Manpower Services Commission and the Equal Opportunities Commission as well as women's organisations and training and education organisers.

The National Women's Register was founded in 1960 following a letter to *The Guardian*'s women's page suggesting that women 'with a desire to remain individuals' should put their name on a register so that they could contact one another. Now with 20,000 members, the Register has one rule - that its members meet to discuss topics of a 'non-domestic nature'. Although not aimed at professional women alone, the group organises local meetings and conferences and, according to the NWR 'friendships flourish, education is possible and self-development is inevitable'.

> 'Women are equal but different. They have different skills that organisations need to capitalise on.'

A more formal structure and a very different service is on offer from Domino Training, a training consultancy and distance learning company which has as its flagship its Women into Management project. Geraldine Brown, the company's managing director, designs, develops and delivers women's training packages aimed at both organisations and individuals. Workshops cover such topics as communicating, self-assertion and creating a positive self-image.

The company can also provide Women into Management 'packs' for companies who do not want to send their female employees on courses - the packs provide all that is required to run the workshops in-house.

The distance-learning programme consists of 12 modules, with self-assessment text books and audio tapes for women who wish to rise to management positions. 'What we have now is the approach that women are equal but different', says

Geraldine Brown. 'They have different skills to offer and they are skills that organisations need to capitalise on. The talk about national skills shortages sounds hollow when we consider the number of women at work whose skills are clearly not being used. If organisations were really concerned about having money they would train women for management posts who would repay the investment many times over.'

Brown is also UK representative for the European Women's Management Development Network, which aims to work co-operatively with national organisations concerned with the development of women's management in countries throughout Europe.

These are just a few of the organisations which can, in different ways, help women either by providing training or by putting them in touch with a network of other women to support and encourage their career development. None of the groups we have mentioned so far are specifically aimed at the computer industry, but there is an increasing number of such groups which use a variety of methods to bring together women from the IT industries and encourage an increase in their numbers.

WOMEN IN COMPUTING GROUPS

Microsyster was founded in 1982, and grew out of Women in Computing, a group set up in 1979, to discuss the impact of information technology on women. It was funded by the London Boroughs Grant Scheme.

Microsyster aims to help women in the computer industry as well as those trying to enter it by providing advice on training and consultancy. One of its most powerful roles is in giving support to women who are having difficulties in their jobs or who need encouragement and confidence-boosting, particularly if they work in a unsympathetic all-male environment, which unfortunately is still often the case. The group also designs its own software and gives advice to women's groups who want to buy a microcomputer.

There are also a number of Women's Computer Centres throughout the country, which, provide hands-on experience for women unfamiliar with computers, and visit schools and groups to talk about opportunities for women in computing and how to go about pursuing them. Many of these groups were originally funded by the European Social Fund or by local councils, and your council will be able to advise you of any in your area.

HEALTH

Like all health issues, the risk to women working with computing is an emotive issue and one which seems to come and go from the public eye with a sickening regularity.

When VDUs (visual display units) were first introduced, little was known about the long-term effects of working with them and little attention was paid to the psychological and ergonomic issues connected with them. Since then, much research has been done and there have been some frightening and often sensationalist reports about the dangers of working with VDUs.

It was also found that women were more likely to be at risk than men. Female workers tend to use VDUs for longer periods than men, being employed in intensive clerical-type jobs which involve word processing, data processing and information retrieval.

Health risks from the use of visual display units only apply to women who work in front of a screen for very long periods over a very long time

The two most common worries to women working with computers for long periods are VDU eyestrain, which can cause severe headaches and sickness, and the risk of miscarriage to pregnant women. Other causes of concern have been hazards caused by radiation, cataracts, dermatitis, fatigue and mental tiredness and stress.

Fortunately, these risks only apply to women who work in front of a screen for very long periods over a very long time. Even then the risk is quite small. The suspected incidence of miscarriage of babies to women who work with computers while pregnant or even before they conceive is very low.

Marilyn Davidson and Cary Cooper of the University of Manchester Institute of Science and Technology (UMIST), discussing the reported pregnancy difficulties in the late 1970s in Canada, the UK and the US, claim that 'it is difficult to assume a linkage between VDU work and miscarriage on such limited sample sizes'.

Also, research into these areas has developed so rapidly that there is now no need for women to be put at risk at all. Manufacturers of VDUs have developed screens which are much easier on the eye, and health, psychological, social and ergonomic considerations are all made at the point of manufacture.

Recommendations for women working with computers for long periods now include:

* A pace of work suitable to the individual
* Regular breaks from the job
* The possibility of changing jobs so that one person does not
   sit at a screen for any length of time
* Comfortable working conditions
* Opportunites for training and development
* Education about the work process and the equipment used

With the evolution of the modern 'paper-less' office, much thought is now put into office and workplace design with an emphasis on lighting, seating and environment which was not considered necessary in offices which did not use computers.

In fact, surveys have shown that although in the early days VDU workers experienced headaches, fatigue and stress, others found that working with computers added to the enjoyment of their job and relieved them of many mundane tasks which had previously made their work stressful and tiring.

The British Health and Safety Executive takes the attitude that health and safety problems for VDU workers are very low, and can largely be overcome by a change in working patterns and improved working conditions by both employers and designers of workstations and office furniture.

If you are concerned about any risks to your health through your work, you should visit your doctor, consult your personnel manager or trade union official, or talk to your manager

However, this is not to underestimate the seriousness of the problem. If you are concerned about any risks to your health through your work, for whatever the reason, you must do something about it.

Visit your doctor, and consult your personnel manager or trade union official if you have one, or talk to your manager. Organisations such as the National Computing Centre will be able to advise you on the latest research findings into the subject.

Trade unions, especially APEX, have carried out extensive research into this area and will also be able to help. Alternatively the women's computing groups listed above will be able to advise you. Any responsible employer will immediately put your fears at rest.

DAY-TO-DAY PROBLEMS

Although nothing is more important than your health, there are many other problems that women can face in the course of their work which may seem trivial, but can still affect the way they work and their development.

Travel

Travel is one of the problems. In today's computer industry, travelling domestically or internationally is considered to be part of the job. We have already heard successful women talk about how they can wake up one day in New York and the next in Paris. Living and working at such a pace is not easy for anyone, but even travelling alone on a much more mundane scale can be fraught with problems for women: even a journey on the '125' train from London to Birmingham.

Until male attitudes to working women change, women will continue to be patronised and pestered by male travellers

A woman alone is vulnerable. Any woman who has ever gone into a hotel bar or restaurant on her own will know the infuriating sidelong glances, the barman's knowing smile, the stares and the general suspicion she arouses.

Any woman who has ever travelled alone on a plane or train will be familiar with the patronising chats she has to endure from fellow (male) passengers while male business travellers are left, unpestered, to get on with their reading or work; not to mention the general indifference of air hostesses who fawn on male passengers. (I once flew first class from New York to San Francisco on a business trip. I was the only woman on the flight, and I was the only person not to be offered a drink.)

Until male attitudes to working women change, these

situations will continue. However, the hotel industry at least is wakening up to the fact that its business guests are no longer mainly male. The Crest Group, for example, now offers 'Women's Rooms' on women-only floors. The rooms offer security and special attention as well as extras such as hair-dryers, tights, toiletries and other special facilities for women travellers which are not usually provided. Staff are also trained to cater for the needs of business women.

Similarly there is an increasing number of small, private hotels which sell themselves as 'ideal for women'. These hotels, such as Pride of Britain's 'Town Houses' are discreet places which look like private homes but which offer the comfort and privacy which is not always found in large, impersonal hotel chains.

There are still many countries in the world, especially in the Far and Middle East, where a woman's presence at a business meeting is considered unusual, and the woman many find herself ignored or even insulted

International travel poses different problems. There are still many countries in the world, especially in the Far and Middle East, where a woman's presence at a business meeting is considered unusual, to say the least, and the woman may find herself being ignored or even insulted.

As advancing technology encircles an ever-shrinking world, we can only hope that these attitudes will change, too. However, the 'they won't like it if we send a woman' argument is not sufficiently strong to prevent a woman persevering in the face of what may seem indomitable odds.

Many women have faced up to difficult situations in countries where women do not usually participate in business, and they have come out well, winning the respect of colleagues from all over the world.

Remember: nothing will change if no-one tries to change it!

Sexism

Although on paper there may be no real obstacles to women progressing up the career ladder in the same way as their male colleagues, in practice this is not always the case. No matter how well-meaning an employer, regardless of their equal opportunities policies or statements on encouraging women, it is a woman's immediate colleagues that can often cause the most problems.

Bottom pinching and suggestive remarks, however nauseating, may have a Benny Hill-style innocence and most of the people who are guilty of these things defend their actions by saying they are 'just a bit of fun' and 'harmless'. The woman who objects to such things is a miserable creature who can't take a joke.

The main weapon that a woman can arm herself with to fight sexual harassment or sexist treatment is knowledge

These actions are harmless for them, yes. Especially if they continue to get away with it. But for a woman, being treated as a frivolous, trivial object when she is trying to do a serious, responsible job only makes difficult things impossible.

Since 1976, and the passing of the Sex Discrimination Act, it has been illegal for a woman to be treated less favourably than a man would in similar circumstances. It is, however, not always easy to enforce this law.

ACAS (The Advisory, Conciliation and Arbitration Service) will advise, but a recent study showed that only 40 per cent of such complaints were ever brought before an industrial tribunal, many being settled out of court or just abandoned.

The main weapon that a woman can arm herself with if she is being treated in a sexist way, suffering sexual harassment or feels her progress is being hindered purely because of her sex, is knowledge. If she acquaints herself with her rights, she will be in a stronger position to enforce them. She must also persevere, and be determined to win, if she is not going to be ground down. Help is available from a variety of sources; women's groups, trade unions, ACAS and of course personnel departments.

If, however, the problems persist or are extreme, the Equal Opportunities Commission will investigate the issue. Cases of sexual discrimination have also been known to go to the European Court of Human Rights if satisfaction is not obtained through our own legal system.

CHAPTER 8

What Does the Future Hold?

The factors which make the computing industry seem unwelcoming to women. The need for a change in emphasis. Looking for new ways to encourage women into the industry. A new era in computing?

This is an exciting time for women in business, and for women in computing in particular. Their true value and potential is slowly being realised, and many steps are being taken to ensure that theycontribute to its future.

In this book we have spoken to a number of successful women; women who have made it, often against all odds, and carved themselves a position in the computing industry. But it would be misleading to suggest that all women in computing share their experiences. We have not dwelt on the cases - and there are

A female managing director is usually an exceptional person; a male managing director is not necessarily so

many - where women have failed to achieve career success, and it is not the purpose of this book to do so.

Women do not succeed for many reasons, and no-one could suggest that they fail simply because they are women. But certainly there is evidence that women, much more than men, suffer in a business environment from lack of confidence, lack of support, lack of encouragement, lack of training and poor incentives; together with social and emotional pressures these factors often combine to make the climb up the career ladder an arduous one. A female managing director is usually an exceptional person; a male managing director is not necessarily so.

The steps that are being taken now to encourage more women to enter the computer industry are aimed at solving an urgent problem which is expected to be with us for some time, that of a shortage of skilled computer staff in a rapidly expanding information technology industry.

These measures are laudable, but they are not aimed specifically at the even longer term problem of improving women's standing in business, although hopefully they will have this knock-on effect.

The Women into IT Campaign is the main focus of activity at the moment. The Campaign is based on overcoming the obstacles of shortages of skilled staff which has been exacerbated by the contracting technical graduate pool on which the computer industry has historically relied. The problems associated with staff shortages cannot be underestimated; according to the Women into IT professionals - and an estimated requirement for more than 50,000 over the next five years.

The Women into Technology Campaign estimates that there will be a requirement for more than 50,000 computer professionals over the next five years

The rate of entry of girls to professional and technician careers has halved over the past six years, and 'the absolute numbers were falling even before the demographic down-turn began', according to the Women into IT Campaign.

It also states that 'the situation is considerably worse in England and Wales than in Scotland, France, the United States or the Far East. If English girls entered and sustained IT related careers in the same proportion as American, French or Singaporean girls there would be no current or prospective shortage of trainees.'

This is interesting; apparently women form a greater proportion of the British Computer Society's overseas membership than they do of its UK membership, because 50 per cent of computer science graduates of Chinese and Indian origin in Malaysia, Singapore and Indonesia are female. Also, overseas students on UK computing courses of Indian or Chinese origin account for a large proportion of female students.

One of the reasons given for this is that Asian businesses are often run by families, with all members participating, and Asian women have traditionally carried out accounting and book-keeping type roles, and the transition to working with computers is, for them, an obvious one.

But what is going wrong in this country? Education, as we have discussed, lies at the beginning of the problem, but it does not rest with it. However, the Women into IT report claims that the education system and not employers is almost entirely to blame.

Fewer girls are taking computer as an option whether it be at GCSE or degree level, and so employers, claims the report, find it difficult to recruit more than 20 per cent of trainees who are women, with some exceptions, such as ICL which last year managed to achieve 30 per cent.

Having said that, the report also points out that two-thirds of IT employers do not recruit trainees at all, and those that do often use methods designed to select from among young male graduates, hoping to attract 'technically-minded, money motivated, job-hopping' males.

There are also few IT employers who have routines for part-time or home-workers, as we have discussed.

These factors combine to make computing appear an industry which does not welcome women, and one which women are not attracted by. At school girls find computing packaged with mathematics, science and 'boys' subjects', and out in the business world they see it as a 'euphemism for word processing'.

At the same time they see newspaper advertisements for professional IT jobs aimed at square-jawed, mobile, independent males with technical brains. It is hardly surprising that women now account for over half of law graduates. These subjects appear much more attractive and much more suited to their skills than does computing.

A CHANGE IN EMPHASIS

So far, few employers have not been convinced of the need to change their attitudes. Many do not see the solution to their problem of staff shortages lying with the recruitment of women. Those that do see it, do not know or are reluctant to admit that their present recruitment practices are male-oriented. They are even more reluctant to invest hard cash in facilities such as creches, or reorganise their methods by introducing home-working or part-time working practices.

And yet these are often the same companies that will pay well over the odds to headhunt a small number of computing professionals to carry out their work.

The Women into IT report suggests, however, that the scale and nature of its findings and recommendations will persuade employers of the need for radical action. There has been great support from employers for the study, and many appear to be actively looking at ways to invest in training and are considering cooperating with other companies in an effort to rectify the situation.

EDUCATION - JOBS FOR THE GIRLS

Many projects are planned to encourage girls of school age to pursue careers in computing. These include visits to schools from IT professionals, seminars, videos, articles in magazines and TV programmes. Competitions will be run with a view to involving computing within subjects which girls are likely to enjoy - such as one for Craft Design and Technology departments to develop a Campaign logo, and one for the best script and video produced by schoolgirls to illustrate what life is like for an IT professional, being run jointly with the BBC. The hope is that girls will become interested in computing, and not the film industry!

Plans are also afoot to make contact with women reading non-IT subjects at university and polytechnic, and to show them how their skills and interests can be developed within an IT career.

In America, businesses and employers have a greater level of contact with higher education than we do here; this has proved to be a successful way of involving students in business, and one which UK companies are being urged to adopt.

RECRUITMENT TECHNIQUES - CHER-CHEZ LA FEMME

In the 1960s, the computer industry needed programmers for languages which are today losing popularity. Employers looking for programmers for languages such as Cobol and Assembler used aptitude tests to choose candidates. These days the swing is away from this style of computing and staff are needed more in areas such as user support, systems analysis and project management.

Aptitude tests of the old school are less relevant. And so there is a great need for employers to experiment with new ways of choosing their computing staff and spend more time identifying efficient ways of testing them.

There has also been a general feeling within the computer industry that there is only one way to achieve career success, and that is through the traditional route from programmer to systems analyst and so on. But as numbers contract, other ways of progressing up the computing ladder are being considered.

When people actually start to look, there are hundreds of women lurking in hidden corners of the country who are more than able to fill the vacancies that exist

The Women into IT report quotes several recent DEC sales training courses which included 30 per cent former secretaries among the participants. This is obviously not a common occurrence, but it does show that women from clerical backgrounds can be retrained in other areas, if they are given the chance and the encouragement.

When people actually start to look, there are hundreds of women lurking in hidden corners of the country who are more than able to fill the vacancies that exist.

Pilot 'returner' workshops are underway which aim to attract part-time trainees without any previous IT experience, as well as attracting women back into computing who have left to bring up a family. Even Army wives living in isolated areas have been identified; many of these women speak a foreign language, many live away from centres of employment and many could be employed by using remote working methods.

Creches, flexible working hours and help for women looking after children or elderly relatives are all being looked at with new eyes; not as ridiculous perks, but as business necessities.

After years of being treated as second-class citizens in the job market, women are being pursued as if they were an endangered species

Most important of all, the psychological problems that hinder women when they enter computing are being analysed in a scientific way for perhaps the first time.

The report suggests a variety of projects, including the establishment of support networks, awareness seminars, professional development activities aimed just at women.

It also recommends the creation of a database of relevant courses and materials, competitions and awards for organisations who do the most to enhance the professional development of their own IT staff, and the production of case studies based on existing experiences.

Companies are being encouraged to develop their own methods of monitoring their progress. The products are dramatic and serious. Will they work?

Most computer firms have risen to the challenge and many have policies planned or underway to bring more women into the industry. ICL, IBM, Bull and many, many more have shown definite enthusiasm.

UK firms committed nearly £80,000 to the Women into IT project and the Government pledged £20,000. Time will tell how successful these efforts will be.

The people on the receiving end of all this sudden attention -the women themselves - could be excused for feeling rather baffled by it all. After years of being treated as second-class citizens in the job market they are now being pursued and wooed as if they were an endangered species.

'It's all very admirable,' said one young programmer. 'But as computing opens up to women, so do many other industries. Many of my female friends are pursuing careers in finance, for example, because this seems an exciting profession, and a well-paid one. Most of them use computers in the course of their job anyway, so there is nothing amazing about working with computers.'

'Big accountancy firms used to be predominantly male, but now there are hundreds of girls going into accountancy. They think my job is boring and mechanical - not creative. I suppose its because they don't understand exactly what I do, but it is also because they think they will reach senior positions within their profession long before I do, and they may be right.'

But it is not too late for the computer industry, and it is certainly not too late for women. They now have more choice than ever before, and more opportunity.

BRAVE NEW WORLD

Industry will be able to benefit enormously from the wealth of talent commanded by women, and the women themselves can walk with confidence through the doors that have now been opened. We hope that it is not too late to convince them of the many advantages of working in this business.

All the skills that women have - management, logic, creativity, organisation - make them ideal candidates for senior positions within the computer industry.

A recent newspaper article quoted Dr Cary Cooper, of the Manchester School of Management at UMIST, who has researched extensively into this subject, and who notes that women, with their instinct to look after not only themselves but their families too, makes them superior to men as managers, and also gives them a clearer sense of perspective.

The professional woman works for self-fulfilment; she enjoys being valued by her colleagues and feeling that she is making a contribution. And this attitude leads to less stress at work; stress-related illness rates are much lower among women.

Hopefully, the projects presently underway represent the start of a new era in computing, where sexual prejudice becomes as much a part of the past as punched cards

All of the women I have spoken to in this book have had different experiences and different careers: they are different people. No-one can claim that one woman's life will be the same as another, or that one woman's strengths and weaknesses are those of all women.

Grouping women together - even for the purposes of this book - is often misleading. Many women positively recoil from 'women's issues' and prefer to make their own way on the battleground, meeting men on their own terms. This has in the past been the only way for them to get on, and even now there is no evidence that women in industry are going to have it easy, although some of the prejudices that had previously added to their handicap are being whittled away, slowly but surely.

But the measures that we have seen here, aimed at solving an economic problem, are not aimed at making life pleasant for women. They will still have to face innumerable obstacles in their working lives, and no amount of private or government funding is going to change basic human attitudes overnight.

We must hope, however, that the projects presently underway represent the start of a new era in computing, where sexual prejudice becomes as much a part of the past as punched cards.

It is a pity, for the computer industry's own sake, that it did not hold these fine principles twenty years ago, when women were coming out of the universities and colleges bright-eyed and bushy-tailed, ready for the brave new world. Computing, then just poised for take-off, could have harnessed this energy and become an industry as ahead of its time as many of its technical innovations.

APPENDIX 1

The Women into IT Campaign

The Report of the 'Women into IT' Campaign
Feasibility Study - Management Summary

The popular view that information technology is exclusively the domain of male 'technofreaks' or a euphemism for word-processing has led to a computer industry largely dominated by males.

The government and many computer companies have grouped together behind a national Women into Information Technology campaign (WIT) to change this biased situation, and reduce the well-publicised skills shortage.

As a result a WIT report has been produced which is aimed at showing employees the current problem and indicating how more women can be attracted to work in the computer industry.

As well as trying to reverse the decline of girls and young women into IT related courses, WIT seeks to encourage employers to organise 'returner' programmes to make it easier for women who have taken a career break, or have demonstrated aptitude in another area of work, to make the move into IT related work.

The Women into IT Report was published on 1st March 1989. It shows what employers are doing to encourage women into the computer industry.

The Report's conclusions are shown on the following pages:

1 The Problem

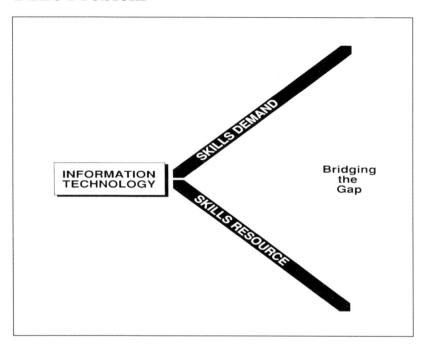

* Shortages of skilled staff are far and away the most significant obstacle to the more widespread and effective use of IT and have been for the past five years.

* Those shortages are becoming more serious as the numbers entering the industry increasingly fail to meet a growing demand.

* The 'A' level and Technical Graduate pool which the IT industry has relied on heavily for its trainee intake has been contracting and will do so more rapidly in the future.

* The competition from other professions for recruits from this pool also continues to increase.

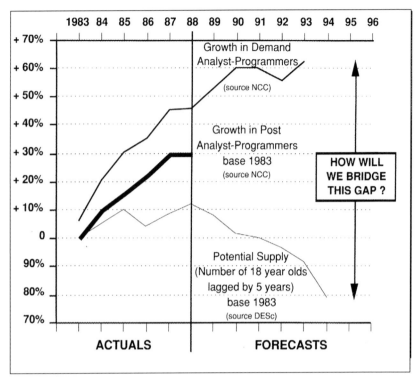

* This recruitment pool does not appear to adequately match the aptitude and skills profiles which is required to effectively develop and use today's IT based products and services let alone those of tomorrow.

* As a proportion of entrants to professional and technician grade careers in IT, the rate of entry of girls and women has halved over the past six years . The absolute numbers were falling even before the demographic down-turn took effect.

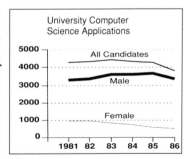

* The situation is considerably worse in England and Wales when compared with Scotland, France, the United States or the Far East. If English girls entered and sustained IT related careers in the same proportion as American, French or Singaporean girls there would be no current or prospective shortage of trainees. In Japan girls also form a higher proportion of those entering technical and professional grade IT training than in the United Kingdom.

2 The Causes

* Two-thirds of IT employers do not currently recruit trainees and those who do often use methods designed to select from young male technical graduates, seen as the most mobile group of the population.

* Similar attitudes tend to prevail in the selection and recruitment of experienced staff.

* Most IT employers' working conditions and staff development paths are designed to attract technically oriented young males.

* Computing is frequently taught in schools and colleges in ways which positively discourage girls from showing or sustaining interest.

* Many careers advisors actively route girls towards traditional 'women-oriented' jobs and away from the opportunities available in the field of Information Technology.

3 The Opportunities

* Most of the predicted IT jobs of the future will demand business aptitudes, people-oriented skills and 'multi-

tasking' management potential more than technical ability. Those aptitudes and skills are frequently better developed on the courses and careers into which girls and women have been entering in increasing numbers and proportions over recent years. These include business studies, office administration, marketing, accountancy and law.

* There is a large pool of under-utilised women in the 25 to 45 age group, many of whom have demonstrated the above aptitudes and abilities. Some will have done so in current positions, others before taking a career break. The flexibility of working arrangements that a well organised IT operation can offer provides a major attraction for career enhancement or returner moves for many women.

4 The Feasibility Study

* In January 1988, growing awareness of the problem caused IT Skills Agency to launch a Feasibility Study to discover whether a campaign to encourage more women to enter IT related careers could be a solution.

* The Study was supported by the Department of Trade and Industry and organised through the IT Skills Agency with the assistance of the British Computer Society, the Equal Opportunities Commission, the National Computing Centre and the National Economic Development Office. The contributors included British Petroleum, BOC Training, Digital Equipment Company, Electronic Data Systems, Exell, F.I. Group, Ferranti, IBM, Intel, Istel, Keith London Associates, Littlewoods, the Post Office, Research Machines, STC Group (including ICL), Unilever and numerous ITEC's, Colleges of FE, Polytechnics and University departments.

* The support given by industry to the Feasibility Study has

shown that the need for a coherent, credible and well organised campaign to encourage more girls and women to enter and sustain IT related careers is already widely appreciated.

* There is a new willingness among employers to come together to support projects that help meet both their corporate recruitment objectives and national goals. They are becoming well aware of the damage that past, often sub-conscious, recruitment policies have caused.

* While some employers are hesitant about supporting 'women only' projects they relate more positively to those 'designed with women in mind ... men also welcome'.

5 The Campaign Objective

To help employers to overcome current and prospective shortages of IT skilled staff by raising the number and proportion of girls and women entering and sustaining IT related careers at all levels.

6 The Means

By bringing together concerned employers to form collaborative teams organising and running specific projects and by co-ordinating those projects into a national 'Women into Information Technology' (WIT) campaign.

The Campaign should include:

* Projects to improve vocational education and careers advice in schools and make it clear to teachers and pupils alike that it is acceptable, normal, worthwhile and exciting for girls to enter and sustain IT related careers.

* Projects to enhance recruitment into IT trainee posts from non-technical students (most of whom are now female) at all levels from non-graduate to post-graduate.

* The identification and dissemination of selection and recruitment methods that are in tune with employers' requirements for a trainee intake with a more appropriate mix of aptitudes.

* Projects to open up the natural career path from office administration to departmental computing, including ensuring the development and provision of the necessary training and experience modules.

* Returner recruitment and training programmes on a scale similar to those currently provided for 16 - 25 year old first career entrants.

* Programmes to make effective use of able but isolated groups (eg armed forces dependants), with both technical and language abilities of the type needed to exploit the 1992 opportunities.

* Programmes of information and encouragement to increase the interest in IT careers among girls and women of all ages.

What Next

Subsequent to the publication of the report those involved in the Feasibility Study are proceeding with industry funded pilot projects designed to both meet specific objectives for the participants and to gain experience for a government supported campaign. They have formed the 'Women into IT Foundation' with the objectives of:

* promoting open and equal education, training, employment and career development opportunities with regard to IT related careers.

* identifying and removing artificial barriers of age or gender with regard to education and training for, and employment and career development in, IT supply and user industries.

* improving the provision of flexible education and training courses and recruitment and career progression programmes which are designed with the needs of women in mind.

* improving the provision of information, guidance and other services to employers who seek to broaden the base from which they recruit staff to handle the micro-electronics, computing, control, communications and other information handling technologies.

* improving the provision of information, guidance and other services to women of all ages who wish to enter employment and pursue careers which involve working with the microelectronics, computing, control, communications and information handling technologies.

Projects already under way include a national competition for the best IT careers video produced by girls under 18 years; an exercise to encourage more Arts and Language graduates to apply for IT trainee posts; 'Returner' and 'Career Enhancement' workshops.

Government was asked to support the cost of co-ordinating these and other projects into a national campaign. The level of such funding is expected to be dependent on the scale and nature of the employer commitment to projects designed not only to meet their own objectives but also to contribute nationally.

Why should employers join the Women into IT Foundation?

Employer should join out of enlightened self-interest. The 1988 recruitment round was a disaster for many employers. But it was only the beginning of the demographic down-turn which will result in a decline of one-third in the number of school-leavers and graduates entering the job-market by the mid-1990s. Helping to foster interest in IT careers amongst the many girls and women not currently attracted will greatly aid your recruitment. Participating in the planned career enhancement and returner programmes will greatly aid your retention programmes.

What does it cost?

Employers wanting to support the Campaign can join in one of two ways.

1) A supporter subscription is £250 p.a. You will receive notice of all events and planned projects and regular progress reports.

2) Full participating membership costs rather more depending on the number and nature of the working parties and projects in which you wish to actively join. Most current participants have already committed in the range £5,000 to £25,000. Some are known to be planning significantly larger investments to support projects intended to yield them hundreds of additional good quality trained and motivated staff.

For further information for employers, individuals and providers of education, training and careers advice contact: Ellen Neighbour, WIT Administrator, c/o Slough Itec, 5 - 7 Colndale Road, Colnbrook, Slough, Berkshire SL3 OHQ.

APPENDIX 2

Useful Names and Addresses

ACAS
(Head Office)
27 Wilton Street
London SWlX 7AZ
Tel: (01) 210 3600

ACAS
(London Regional Office)
Clifton House
83 Euston Road
London NW1 2RB
Tel: (01) 388 5100

APEX
(Head Office)
22 Worple Road
London SW19 4DF
Tel: (01) 947 3131

British Computer Society
13 Mansfield Street
London W1M OBP
Tel: (01) 637 0471

British Federation of University Women
Crosby Hall
Cheyne Walk
London SW3 5BA
Tel: (01) 352 5354

The City Women's Network
59 Coleman Street
London EC2

Domino Training
(Women into Management)
56 Sharnwood Road
Shepshed
Leicestershire LE12 9NP
Tel: 0509 505404

Engineering Careers Information Service
54 Clarendon Road
Watford
Hertfordshire WD1 1LB
Tel: 0923 38441

The Engineering Council
10 Maltravers Street
London WC2R 3ER
Tel: (01) 240 7891

Engineering Industry
Training Board
54 Clarendon Road
Watford
Hertfordshire WD1 1LB
Tel: (0923) 38441

Equal Opportunities Commission
Overseas House
Quay House
Manchester M3 3HN
Tel: 061 833 9244

Equal Opportunities Commission
The Training Agency
Moorfoot
Sheffield S1 4PQ
Tel: 0742 753 2775

The Industrial Society
(Pepperell Unit)
17-23 Southampton Row
London WC1B 5HA
Tel: (01) 831 8388

Information Technology
Skills Agency
CBI Education Foundation
Centre Point
103 New Oxford Street
London WC1A 1DU
Tel: (01) 379 7400

Manufacturing Science and
Finance (MSF)
79 Camden Road
London NW1 9ES
Tel: 01 267 4422

National Advisory Centre
on Careers for Women
8th Floor
Artillery House
Artillery Row
London SW1P 1RT
Tel: (01) 799 2129

National Computing Centre
Limited (NCC)
(Head Office)
Oxford Road
Manchester M1 7ED
Tel: 061-228 6333

The National Women's Register
245 Warwick Road
Solihull
West Midlands B92 7AH

Alisa Swarbrick
The Open University
Women in Technology
Project Department
11 Fairfax House
Merrion Street
Leeds LS2 8JU
Tel: (0532) 444431

Thames Polytechnic
Wellington Street
Woolwich
London SE18 6PF
Tel: (01) 854 2030

United Kingdom Federation
of Business and
Professional Women
23 Ansdell Street
London W8 5BN
Tel: (01) 938 1729

The Women's Computer
Centre
Wesley House
Wild Court
London WC2
Tel: (01) 430 0112

Women's Engineering
Society
c/o Imperial College of
Science and Technology
Department of Civil
Engineering
Imperial College
Exhibition Road
London SW7 2BY
Tel: (01) 589 5111

Women into Engineering
Centre
Southbank Technology
Park, London Road
London SE1 6LN
Tel: (01) 922 8876

Women into Engineering,
Science and Technology
(WEST)
83 Fordwych Road
London NW2 3TL

Women into Management
(WIM)
64 Marryat Road
Wimbledon
London SW19 5BN
Tel: 01 946 1238

The Women's Returners Net-
work
c/o Hatfield Polytechnic
PO Box 109
College Lane
Hatfield
Hertfordshire
Tel: Hatfield 79000

Women in Science and En-
gineering
c/o Engineering Council
10 Maltravers Street
London WC2R 3ER
Tel: (01) 240 7891

Women in Technology in
the European Community
(WITEC)
c/o The Centre for Continu-
ing Vocational Education
Sheffield University
65 Wilkinson Street
Sheffield S10 2GJ
Tel: 0742 768653

Women and Training
GLOSCAT
Oxstalls Lane
Gloucester

APPENDIX 3

Recommended Reading

ASSOCIATION OF PROFESSIONAL, EXECUTIVE, CLERI-
CAL AND COMPUTER STAFF (APEX), *New Technology: a
Health and Safety Report*, 1985.

BIRD, Emma, *Information Technology in the Office; the
Impact on Women's Jobs*, Manchester Equal Opportunities
Commission, 1980.

DAVIDSON, Marilyn and COOPER, Cary L, *Women and
Information Technology*, Wiley, 1987.

DEAKIN, Rose, *Women and Computing: the Golden Opportunity*, Macmillan, 1984.

DICKSON, Ann, *A Woman in Your Own Right*, Quartet, 1985.

FAULKNER, Wendy and ARNOLD, Erik, *Smothered by
Invention: Technology in Women's Lives*, Pluto Press, 1985.

HADJIFOTIOU, Nathalie, *Women and Harassment at Work*,
Pluto Press, 1983.

HUWS, Ursula, *Your Job in the Eighties; a Woman's Guide to
New Technology*, Pluto Press, 1982.

LAUROCHE, Janice and RYAN, Regina, *Strategies for
Women at Work*, Counterpoint, 1984.

McDONALD, Janet, *Climbing the Ladder*, Methuen, 1986.

MARSHALL, Judi, *Women Managers: Travellers in a Male
World*, Wiley, 1984.

NATIONAL COMPUTING CENTRE, *Women and Computing*, 1981.

READ, Sue, *Sexual Harassment at Work*, Hamlyn, 1982.

ROTHSCHILD, Joan, *Machina Ex-dea: Feminist Perspectives on Technology*, Pergamon Press, 1983.

ROTHSCHILD, Joan, *Women, Technology and Innovation*, Pergamon Press, 1982.

STEAD, Bette Ann, *Women in Management*, Prentice Hall, 1982.

STEELE, Maggie and THORNTON, Zita, *aWomen Can Achieve Career Success*, Thorsons, 1988.

STEELE, Maggie and THORNTON, Zita, *Women Can Return to Work*, Thorsons, 1988.

TRADES UNION CONGRESS, *Women and New Technology*, 1984.

INDEX

ACAS, *see* Advisory Conciliation
    and Arbitration Service
Accountancy, 94
Ada, 49, 52
Advisory Conciliation and Arbi-
    tration Service (ACAS), 85,
    86, 108
ANSA, 39-41
APEX, 82, 108,112
    see also Trade unions
Aquino, Corazan, 75
Assembler, 92
Au pairs, 63
    see also Childcare
Australia, 56

Baby '34' and '36', 36, 38
BBC, 91
BCS,*see* British Computer Society
Bhutto, Benazir, 75
BOC Training, 102
Bohl, Marylin (case study), 41-4
Brain drain, 9
British Computer Society, 68, 108
    Schools Working Party, 7
British Federation of University
    Women (BFUW), 19, 108
    see also Women's groups
British Health and Safety Execu-
    tive, 82
    see also Health
British Petroleum, 102
British Telecom, 70
Brown, Geraldine, 78-9
Brussels, 71
Bull, 17, 29, 41, 94
    equal opportunities scheme, 29
    Hemel Hempstead, 30
    'Homeworkers' Scheme, 30, 31
BUPA, 30

California, 9, 44
California Software Products 36-9

Campaign for Workplace Nurser-
    ies, 64
Career breaks, 65-6, 77
Case studies, 24-7, 27-9, 32-3,
    36-9, 39-41, 41-4, 49-4, 49-
    53, 56-75
Childcare, 60, 62-71
    au pairs, 63
    baby boom, 71
    childminders, 63
    in Europe, 60, 70, 71
    maternity leave, 66-7
    nannies, 61-3
    nurseries
    state, 63
    workplace, 63-4
    small firms, 67
    subsidised childcare, 65
City, The, 51, 75
City Women's Network, The, 108
    see also Women's groups
Cobol, 52, 92
Combat games, 7, 12
Communication
    importance of, 44
Computer People, Recruitment
    Agency, 54, 55
    Professional Conduct Book, 55
Computer science applications, uni-
    versity, 100
Conoco Oil, 14
Consultant, 32-3, 53-7
Contracting, 48, 53-7
Cooper, Sir Frank, 51, 95
Council, 80
Creches, 20, 91, 93
    see also Childcare
Crest Group, The, 84

Data Logic, 24, 26, 27
Data Processing (DP), 32-3
Davidson, Marilyn, 81
DB2, 42
DEC, 27, 28, 93, 102

Digital Research (DR), 41, 42, 43
Domino Training, 78, 108

Education 2, 4, 11-22, 92
    open university, 20
    polytechnics, 13-16
    schools, 7, 12-13, 90
    universities, 16-19
    WIT project, 91, 103-5
Electronic Data Systems, 102
Engineering Careers Information
        Service, 108
Engineering Council, 108
Engineering Industry Training
        Board, 108
Entrepreneur, 5, 48
    running your own company, 75
Equal opportunities, 2
    at Bull, 29
Equal Opportunities Board, 3, 84
Equal Opportunities Commission,
        77-8, 86, 108, 109, 112
European Court of Human Rights,
        86
European market, 70-71
European Social Fund, 80
European Women's Management
        Development Network, 79
    see also Women's groups
Evans, Marie (case study), 56-7
Exell, 102

F International, 67-8
Far East, 84, 89
Feminism, 74-5
Ferguson, Ann (case study), 39-41
Ferguson, Bob, 39
Ferranti, 102
F.I. Group, 102
Fleet, Rex, 17, 18, 19
Foster, Joanna, 3
France, 89, 101

GEC, 51
Ghandi, Indira, 75
GLOSCAT
    Women and Training, 110
Gordon, Daphne (case study), 49-
        53
Government, 94
    funding, 96, 102
Graduate Training Schemes, 22
    NCR, 18-19
Guardian, The, 78

Halbot, Sue, 68
Health, 74, 80-82
    British Health and Safety Execu-
        tive, 82
    checklist for working with com-
        puters, 81
    working with VDUs, 80-82
High Integrity Systems (HIS), 49
Homeworkers, 8, 21, 66, 67-70, 91
Honeywell Bull, see Bull
Hotels, 84

IBM, 14, 15, 27, 41, 42, 43, 94, 102
    Systems '34' and '36', 40
ICL, 61, 64, 94
    CBS division, 68
    working party, 61-2, 64, 75
ITT, 50, 51
IMS, 42
Imperial Tobacco, 32-33
Industrial Society, 109
    Pepperell Unit, 61, 77
Information Technology (IT)
        Skills Agency, 109
    Survey, 4
Intel, 102
Interviews, 17, 24, 60
Istel, 102

Japan, 40, 101

Job-sharing, 70

Keith London Associates, 102

Labour Research Department, 76
Lank, Elizabeth, 61, 62, 65, 68, 69, 70, 75
Lancaster University, 17-18
Latin America, 40
Littlewoods, 102
London Boroughs Grant Scheme, 79

Manchester Institute of Science and Technology, University of, (UMIST), 81
Manufacturing Science and Finance (MSF), 109
Manpower Services Commission, 20, 78
Marketing
    a success story, 24-7, 36-40
Marconi, 50
Maternity leave, 66-7
Maternity allowance/pay, 66
Meyer, Golda, 75
Michelin Company, 25
Microsyster, 79-80
    see also Women's groups
Middle East, 84
Milk round, 17
Mobil Data Services, 21
Morton, Pam, 14-16

Nannies, 61-3
    see also Childcare
National Advisory Centre on Careers for Women, 109
National Children's Bureau, 25
National Computing Centre, 82, 109, 112

National Women's Register, 78, 110
    see also Women's groups
NCR, 17, 18
Newman, Christine (case study), 32-3
1992, 70-71
Nurseries
    see also Childcare
    state, 63
    workplace, 63-4

Open University, 20
    see also Education
    Women in Technology Department, 109
Opportunities, 95
    going it alone, 49-53
    grabbing them, 26-7, 29, 53
    sales and marketing, 39-41

Part-time work, 69, 91
Personnel
    success in, 27-9
    departments, 70, 76, 86
Polytechnics, 13-16
    Thames, 13, 109
    see also Education
Post Office, The, 102
'Pregnant Programmers', 68
Professional Conduct, 55
Profit-sharing scheme, 30
Programmer, 15-16, 21, 24, 48, 49
Problems, 83-6
    personal sacrifices, 52-3
    sexism, 85-6
    travel, 83-4

Rashid, Sahidah, 15, 16
Raytheon, 26
Research Machines, 102
Returner schemes, 93

Richell, Liz (case study), 36-9

Sales
    success in, 19, 39-40
Schools, 7, 12-13, 90
    WIT project, 91, 103-5
Scotland, 89, 101
Self-employed, 48
Sex Discrimination Act, 85
Sexual harassment, 74, 76, 85
Sexism, 36, 50, 60, 83-5
    pressures, 12
Shirley, Steve, 67-8
Singapore, 2, 8, 89, 101
Skills shortage, 4, 88-91
    diagram, 100
Slough, 38
Smedley, Sally (case study), 27-9
STC Group, 102
STC machine, 24
Success
    in marketing, 24-7, 36-40
    in personnel, 27-9
    in sales, 19, 39-40
Sweden, 71
Sydney, 56

Thames Polytechnic, 13, 109
Thatcher, Margaret, 75
    Britain, 5, 48
Thursday Club, 61
    see also Women's groups
Times, The, 76
Toronto, 38
Trade and Industry, Department
    of, 103
Trade unions, 76, 82-3, 86, 113
    APEX, 82, 108, 112
Travel, 28
    problems, 83-4

United Kingdom Federation of

Business and Professional
    Women, 109
    see also Women's groups
USA, 25, 26
    California, 9, 44
    comparison with UK, 35-45
    education, 92
    skills shortage, 89, 101
    department of defense, 52
Universities, 16-19
    see also Education
    Lancaster University, 17-18
    Manchester Institute of Sci-
        ence and Technology
        (UMIST), 81, 113
    Manchester School of Manage-
        ment, 95
    Open University, 20
University computer science applica-
    tions, 100
Unilever, 102
Unix, 26

VDU (visual display unit), 80-81
Venezuela, 40

Wales, 89, 101
Walsh, Madeleine, 15, 16
Willetts, Flick (case study), 24-7
Women Computer Centre, 80, 109
Women's Engineering Society, 110
Women into Engineering, 6
Women into Engineering
    Centre, 110
    initiative, 6
Women into Engineering, Science
    and Technology (WEST), 110
Women's Groups, 61-2, 76-7, 86
    British Federation of University
        Women, 19, 108
    City Women's Network, The,
        108

Women's Groups - *continued*
  European Women's Management Development Network, 79
  Microsyster, 79-80
  National Women's Register, 78, 110
  Thursday Club, 61, 77
  United Kingdom Federation of Business and Professional Women, 109
Women's Computer Centre, 109
Women into Engineering, 6, 110
Women into Engineering, Science and Technology (WEST), 110
Women's Engineering Society, 110
Women into Management, 77, 110
Women Returners' Network, 77, 110

Women in Science and Engineering, 110
Women in Technology in the European Community (WITEC), 110
Women into IT Campaign, 97-106
Women into Information Technology (WIT), 6, 20, 21, 61, 89-91, 93
Women into Management, 110
Women's Returners Network, 110
Women's roadshow, 16
Women in Science and Engineering, 110
Women in Technology in the European Community (WITEC), 110
Women and Training (GLOSCAT), 110
Word processing, 6
Worldwide situation, 9

COMPUTER WEEKLY PUBLICATIONS

Computer Weekly is the UK's leading weekly computer newspaper which goes to over 112,000 computer professionals each week. Founded in 1967, the paper covers news, reviews and features for the computer industry. In addition, *Computer Weekly* also publishes books relevant to and of interest to its readership.

Publications to date (obtainable through your bookshop or by ringing 01-685-9435/01-661-3050) are:

Aliens' Guide to the Computer Industry by John Kavanagh

In a lucid and light style, leading computer industry writer John Kavanagh discusses how the various parts of the computer industry inter-relate and what makes it tick. Complete with extensive index, the book is invaluable for all who come into contact with the computer industry.

'Business professionals who worry about their grasp of the general computing scene and do not want to be bombarded with jargon and technicalities, will get good value ... an excellent "snapshot" of the companies, the current areas of interest and the problems' *Financial Times*

ISBN 1-85384-012-2   192 pages   Price £9.95

Computer Jargon Explained by Nicholas Enticknap

This is a totally revised, expanded and updated version of our highly successful guide to computer jargon, *Breaking the Jargon*.

This 176 page book provides the context to and discusses 68 of the most commonly used computer jargon terms. Extensively cross-indexed this book is essential reading for all computer professionals, and will be useful to many business people too. '... a useful shield against the constant barrage of impossible language the computer business throws out' *The Independent*

'... a worthwhile investment' *Motor Transport*

ISBN 0-85384-015-7   176 pages   Price £9.95

A Simple Introduction to Data and Activity Analysis by Rosemary Rock-Evans

Successful analysis of business operations is a pre-requisite to building any computer system within a company. Whereas many existing books approach this topic from an academic point of view, this one is the fruit of years of practical analysis in blue chip companies, by a leading consultant.

This book is essential reading for all analysts in the computer industry, and is also recommended for students to given them a taste of the real world of analysis.

ISBN 1-85384-001-7   272 pages   Price £24.95

Low Cost PC Networking by Mike James

The whole area of PC networking is taking off rapidly now. Can you afford to be left behind? Mike James' *Low Cost PC Networking* shows how networking revolutionises the way we use PCs and the tasks that they perform. It also explains how networking goes further than simply linking PCs, and how it enables you to integrate your operations to transform your business.

Chapters cover everything from planning your network and selecting the hardware and software to applications, technicalities and contacts.

ISBN 0-434-90897-5   256 pages   Price £16.95

Open Systems: The Basic Guide to OSI and its Implementation by Peter Judge

We recognise the need for a concise, clear guide to the complex area of computer standards, untrammelled by jargon and with appropriate and comprehensible analogies to simplify this difficult topic. This book, a unique collaboration between *Computer Weekly* and the magazine *Systems International*, steers an independent and neutral path through this contentious area and is essential for users and suppliers and is required reading for all who come into contact with the computer industry.

ISBN 1-85384-009-2   192 pages   Price £12.95

Computer Weekly Book of Puzzlers compiled by Jim Howson

Test your powers of lateral thinking with this compendium of 187 of the best puzzles published over the years in *Computer Weekly*. The detailed explanations of how solutions are reached make this a useful guide to recreational mathematics. No computer is needed to solve these fascinating puzzles.

'... a pleasant collection of puzzles exercises for computer freaks. Actually probably fewer than half the puzzles here need a computer solution ...' *Laboratory Equipment Digest*

ISBN 1-85384-002-5   162 pages   Price £6.95

How to Get Jobs in Microcomputing by John F Charles

As micros proliferate throughout organisations, opportunities for getting jobs in the micro area are expanding rapidly. The author, who has worked with micros in major organisations, discusses how to get started in microcomputing, describes the different types of job available, and offers tips and hints based on practical experience. Ideal for recent graduates, and those already working with minicomputers or mainframes, who are looking towards a career in micros.

ISBN 1-85384-010-6   160 pages   Price £6.95

Considering Computer Contracting? - The Computer Weekly Guide to Becoming a Freelance Computer Professional by Michael Powell

Everybody in the computer industry talks of doubling their salary by going freelance. This book, written by a freelancer, explains how it's done. The topics covered, including how to form your own company, and handling your finance, also make this book useful for people in other industries considering going it alone.

'... is essential reading for anyone considering taking up contract work.' *The Guardian*

ISBN 1-85384-000-9   156 pages   Price £10.95

Selling Information Technology: A Practical Career Guide by Eric Johnson

Selling in IT requires more skill and creativity than selling in any other profession. This essential handbook for IT sales people explains why and provides practical down-to-earth advice on achieving the necessary extra skills. A collaboration between *Computer Weekly* and the National Computing Centre, this book discusses practical career issues, general IT sales issues, and key IT industry developments.

ISBN 0-85012-684-3   244 pages   Price £12.50

IT Perspectives Conference: The Future of the IT Industry

Many nuggets of strategic thought are contained in this carefully edited transcript of the actual words spoken by leading IT industry decision makers at *Computer Weekly*'s landmark conference held late in 1987. The conference was dedicated to discussing current and future directions the industry is taking from four perspectives: supplier perspectives; communications perspectives; user perspectives and future perspectives.

'... makes compelling reading for those involved in the business computer industry' *The Guardian*

'... thought-provoking points and some nice questions put to speakers at the end' *Daily Telegraph*

ISBN 1-85384-008-4   224 pages   Price £45

The Computer Weekly Annual Guide to Resources '89

This extensively indexed book fulfils the computer industry's need for an independent, handy up-to-date reference review signposting and interpreting the key trends in the computer industry and how companies and their products are adapting to them. A key section is an in-depth independent discussion of 200 software and supplier companies, and of leading industry sectors and significant new products.

'... readable, comprehensive overview of the current UK scene ... it's very good.' *The Guardian*

ISBN 1-85384-014-9   352 pages   Price £45